Unique Eats and Eateries

of

CONNECTICUT

THE PEOPLE AND STORIES BEHIND THE FOOD

Library of Congress Control Number: 2020937369

ISBN: 9781681062914

Design by Jill Halpin

Photos by author unless otherwise noted.

Printed in the United States of America
21 22 23 24 25   5 4 3 2

We (the publisher and the author) have done our best to provide the most accurate information available when this book was completed. However, we make no warranty, guarantee, or promise about the accuracy, completeness, or currency of the information provided, and we expressly disclaim all warranties, express or implied. Please note that attractions, company names, addresses, websites, and phone numbers are subject to change or closure, and this is outside of our control. We are not responsible for any loss, damage, injury, or inconvenience that may occur due to the use of this book. When exploring new destinations, please do your homework before you go. You are responsible for your own safety and health when using this book.

Unique Eats and Eateries

of

CONNECTICUT

THE PEOPLE AND STORIES BEHIND THE FOOD

MIKE URBAN

To Ellen

CONTENTS

ACKNOWLEDGMENTS

First, I'd like to express my admiration and sincere thanks to all the restaurants and specialty shops (and their owners and workers) covered in this book. Virtually all my research was performed in the midst of a pandemic, and I witnessed firsthand how all these places struggled and adapted to stay in business and continue to serve their customers with grace and charm during the most difficult time in American restaurant history. From adversity comes perseverance and innovation, and I'm impressed and inspired by the spirit and ingenuity that helped each of these places survive, even thrive, under such difficult conditions. Thanks, and congratulations.

I'd also like to give special thanks to Sylvia Thanas and Nancy Creel, both of whom helped bankroll portions of the research for the book, picking up tabs and providing cheerful companionship along the way.

I send an extraordinary thanks to my dear friend and travel companion, Alan Gross, who came along with me on many culinary adventures, sampling wonderful foods, hobnobbing with owners and servers, and generally being a great guy to share meals with. I'll always cherish our time on the road together.

Finally, to my wife, Ellen, who's always glad to see me return home from gastronomic outings, often with no enthusiasm for dinner. You're my favorite dining companion of all time, and I look forward to many more meals together in Connecticut and wherever else we may wander.

INTRODUCTION

Some 8,000 restaurants call Connecticut home, from fast-food outlets to haute cuisine establishments and everything in between. In addition, several thousand specialty food shops sell such disparate items as cheese, seafood, coffees, spices, ice cream, baked goods, chocolates, and so much more.

This book contains what I consider to be 85 of Connecticut's most unique food emporiums, each one well worth a visit. There's so much to choose from and explore in the diminutive Nutmeg State that you really don't have to travel far to find numerous revelatory and rewarding culinary experiences.

Most of the establishments in the book are mom-and-pop operations, and most have been in business for more than 10 years. I consider these places to be organically unique—that is, they possess homegrown character and originality and are not the creations of restaurant groups, marketing outfits, or public relations firms. (There's nothing wrong with such places, but they're covered quite extensively in newspapers, magazines, and social media platforms—and they often come and go quite quickly.) This book pays homage to those establishments that wear their uniqueness and their longevity like a comfortable, familiar, beloved overcoat.

The eats and eateries contained in this book are organized in a browsable fashion (in other words, no particular order), and there's a regional index in the back of the book, should you wish to explore specific parts of the state. The book is best used as a reference to be consulted from time to time to get ideas for gustatory outings and adventures. If you find even one or two places you didn't know about or hadn't experienced before, then I'll consider my labors a success.

My previous four food books covered all of New England, and this book gave me a chance to do a deep culinary dive into my adopted home state of 30 years. It's been an education and an adventure for me to research and write this book, and I hope you find my thoughts and suggestions worthy of your attention and your dining dollars. *Bon appétit!*

UNIQUE EATS AND EATERIES
OF
CONNECTICUT

THE PEOPLE AND STORIES BEHIND THE FOOD

There's no place quite like The Place.

This may be the most unique restaurant in the entire state. The Place has been around in its current form since 1971, and it is renowned for its wood-fed-fire cooking pit, its tree stumps for seats, its fresh flowers on every table, and its open-air, woodsmoke-fragranced ambiance.

Back in the early 1940s, an old salt named Whitey set up a small stand on Post Road in Guilford and started roasting clams for hungry passersby. Whitey used tree stumps for seats and roasted his clams over an open fire. He employed many local teens at his seasonal operation, and, in 1971, two of those former teen employees, Vaughn and Gary Knowles, bought the stand and gave it a new name: The Place. In the intervening years, the Knowles brothers have expanded the menu, adding lobster, a few kinds of fish, ribeye steak, and grilled veggies.

Virtually all the cooking is done over an 18-foot-long, wood-fed fire pit with iron grates suspended above the flames. Smoke swirls in the air above the pit, adding a pleasant smoky flavor to everything coming off the iron grates. The Place is a totally outdoors operation, though there's a red-and-white tarp that can be pulled over much of the dining area in the event of rain.

Start your meal with an order of roasted clams, a must-have to get the full Place experience. The littlenecks are placed on grates over the fire until they pop open. Be sure to try the Roast Clam Special, which calls for a slathering of cocktail sauce and butter on the clams. You may also order a pound of steamers or wine-and-garlic mussels.

The most popular main course is whole lobster, which is steamed in a pot by the fire's side and then thrown on the grates for a few minutes of smoky infusion. Filets of bluefish, catfish, and salmon are

The iconic menu board at The Place stands some 10 feet tall and tells you all you need to know about the great food here.

Top middle: Outdoor dining on tree stumps and red tabletops makes The Place about as unique as it can be.

Above middle: A couple of orders of the Roast Clam Special, hot off the fire pit and delivered on piping-hot steel grates.

Right: "Put Your Rump on a Stump" is the battle cry throughout the summer at The Place.

wrapped with lemon and butter in aluminum foil and roasted, as is the chicken breast, which comes plain or barbecued. The ribeye steak goes straight over the flames.

The other must-have is the roasted corn, placed in its water-soaked husk on the grates, then dehusked and dipped in a vat of butter. It's hard to have only one.

This place is about as unusual and as fun as dining gets in Connecticut.

901 Boston Post Rd., Guilford; 203-453-9276
theplaceguilford.com

The Place is BYO for alcohol (not soft drinks), and you may bring any side dishes you wish from home.

Home of the state's most authentic mole sauces

Improbably located in a strip mall on Route 25 south of Newtown's main business district, this gem of a restaurant really delivers authentic Mexican cuisine—especially its mole sauces, which have drawn rave reviews for years.

Mexicali Rose is owned by the husband-and-wife team of Marklin and Minerva Hidalgo. They've been creating authentic Mexican food from the Yucatan peninsula in this storefront spot since 1996.

Upon entering through the strip mall storefront, you'll notice an authentic Mexican look and feel immediately. The walls are covered with Mexican kitsch, the tilework on the floor and the counter by the front window are bright and festive, and the tables are a charming mix of mismatched Formica tops.

Every meal here starts with complimentary chips and salsa, and it sets the tone for what's to come. The chips are light, crispy, and authentic in both flavor and form. No Doritos-style mass-produced product here—the chips at Mexicali Rose are the real deal. The salsa is homemade, smoky and spicy, full of character, and comes with a bit of heat. Order a side of guacamole, and you're all set for appetizers. The guac, chips, and salsa are a great setup for what's to come.

Soups include black bean, which is available daily, and a rotating selection of traditional Mexican soups, such as tortilla soup and chili. Salads are hefty and loaded with fresh goodies such as sliced potato, egg, avocado, Mexican cheeses, red onion, and cilantro.

Tacos, quesadillas, fajitas, and burritos come in a variety of flavors, both meat-laden and vegetarian; all are freshly made to order. Daily specials, such as the enchiladas de mole, frequently come bathed in the Hidalgos' famed mole sauces, made from scratch every day in their tiny kitchen. You'll find the specials posted on a whiteboard by

Top left: The restaurant's interior exudes south-of-the-border fun and a bright, festive atmosphere.

Above left: Start your meal with homemade tortilla chips and smoky salsa.

Top middle: A plate of enchiladas bathed in homemade mole sauce and crumbled Mexican cheese and accompanied by refried black beans and rice.

Above middle: The owners have collected and displayed all sorts of colorful kitsch from travels to their homeland.

Right: Mexicali Rose anchors one end of a strip mall south of downtown Newtown.

the cash register, or your server can recite them for you, so be sure to ask about them. They're one of the Rose's highlights.

First-time customers are usually astounded that such good Mexican food comes from this modest, little storefront eatery in a Newtown strip mall. All Connecticut towns should be so lucky to have such a gem nearby.

71 S Main St. #1, Newtown; 203-270-7003
mexicalirosenewtown.com

If you happen to be a fan of Mexican Coca-Cola, which is sweetened from sugar cane instead of high-fructose corn syrup, you'll find some in the cooler in the dining area.

Daily diner surprises from a seasoned chef

O'Rourke's is a place of never-ending surprises, where chef/owner Brian O'Rourke comes up with new specials almost daily, depending on what he finds in the kitchen's cupboards and coolers when he arrives in the morning. There's also an extensive menu of regular items, such as the Dubliner omelet, Irish soda bread, French toast, eggs Mornay, and Brian's Rueben sandwich. And O'Rourke's is one of a handful of places that serves steamed cheeseburgers (a central Connecticut specialty), made in a custom-built steamer in which freshly ground beef and slabs of Irish cheddar cheese are given a super-hot sauna until cooked and melted to perfection.

There's always something baking at O'Rourke's, be it loaves of bread, muffins, biscuits, cookies, or other oven goodies. Upon being seated, patrons are treated to a small plate of bread samples cooked up that day. There's a boundless variety of baked goods coming out of Brian's ovens, and during the holidays, it's a great place to put in an order for wonderful baked goods to take home.

The diner suffered a devastating fire in 2006 that gutted the building and left little hope for resurrection. However, such is the love for O'Rourke's in the Middletown and Wesleyan communities that some $300,000 was raised by citizens and students to help rebuild and reopen. The diner is better than ever and doing just fine these days.

Brian authored a cookbook, *Breakfast at O'Rourke's*, several years ago to great acclaim. The book contains 73 recipes for

There is a strong bond between O'Rourke's and nearby Wesleyan University, with many of the students and faculty frequenting the diner, especially on Saturday mornings.

Top left: O'Rourke's iconic neon sign and curved glass facade with stainless-steel trim are familiar to Middletown residents and diner aficionados everywhere.

Above left: Irish soda bread French toast topped with homemade jams and clotted cream.

Middle: Chef/owner Brian O'Rourke working his magic in the kitchen.

Top right: The Dubliner omelet, filled with corned beef hash and Irish cheddar cheese and topped with Irish bacon.

Above right: O'Rourke's interior was completely redone after the devastating 2006 fire.

baked goods, omelets, French toasts, frittatas, quiches, sauces, side dishes, and more. There's a concluding chapter that combines many of the recipes into 23 inspired breakfasts that will leave your family and guests wowed. Written in a simple, easy-to-follow style, the book is a godsend for those who believe that breakfast is the best meal of the day.

There is no way to describe what specials might await you when you visit O'Rourke's on any given day. Brian frequently steps out of the kitchen and visits his diners throughout the day, handing out small samples from his latest creations in the kitchen. Ask him what he recommends to order, and listen closely to what he says. It's guaranteed you won't be disappointed. We can only hope that this extraordinary diner owner and chef keeps it up for many years to come.

728 Main St., Middletown; 860-346-6101
orourkesmiddletown.com

PARKVILLE MARKET

A modern food plaza rises in an old factory neighborhood.

The Parkville section of Hartford has been through many changes over the years, and one of the best-received is the recently opened Parkville Market. Basically a restaurant bazaar in an old factory building, Parkville Market brings food seekers together under one roof to partake of many different cuisines and beverages.

With I-84 hovering overhead, Parkville Market is popular among city dwellers and suburbanites alike. It's housed in a converted two-story warehouse and has attractive, new board wood sheathing on the outside, giving the building a warm, inviting look. Old delivery bay doors have been converted to glass and trimmed in maroon-stained wood, allowing lots of natural light into the building. Pull off of Park Street, and follow the drive to the parking lot and the main entrance in the back. There's a large patio area in front of the entrance, with picnic tables and a small bandstand scattered about and illuminated with pretty bulb lights strung overhead.

Inside, you'll find some 20 alluring food stands, each with menus hung out front and counter attendees ready to take your order. It's best to stroll the length of the building to check out all the offerings before ordering. A number of popular Hartford-area restaurants are represented here, along with some new surprises. The stands run the length of the hall on both sides, with lots of communal tables in the middle. The upstairs level consists of a lot of semiprivate dining areas, each a separate alcove tricked out with a spacious picnic-style dining table.

The current lineup of food vendors includes Bombay Express (Indian cuisine with a bit of Cantonese), Brazilian Gula Grill (empanadas, grilled meats, yuca potato fries, fresh pineapple

Left: The market's airy space, numerous food stands, and ample indoor and outdoor seating make it a great place to dine.

Right: This plate of Puerto Rican mofongo comes from the restaurant of the same name, which has a popular stand at the market.

salsa), J's Crab Shack (seafood, most of the New England variety), Mofongo (Puerto Rican delights, including an amazing variety of namesake mofongo dishes), Twisted Italian Cafe (fun, funky takes on traditional Italian food), Jamaican Jerk Shack (jerk and curry dishes, including cow foot for the more adventurous), and Hartford Poke Co. (a variety of tasty poke bowls, including a build-your-own). Be sure to check in advance on the market's website to get the current lineup of vendors.

Weather permitting, you may want to take your goodies outdoors to the spacious patio and dine alfresco in one of Hartford's liveliest neighborhoods. Parkville Market is a great way to sample an amazing variety of foods with family and friends in a warm, friendly, lively atmosphere.

1400 Park St., Hartford; 860-470-4511
parkvillemarket.com

Outdoor live concerts are regular events in warmer months on Parkville's spacious patio in front of the food hall.

The joys of Colombian cuisine hiding in plain sight

Well inland from South Norwalk's trendy restaurant row is a modest Colombian gem hidden at one end of a strip mall on New Canaan Road. Antojos has been serving up delectable Colombian fare since 2016, and it has deservedly built a loyal clientele of Colombian locals and others savvy enough to seek this place out and partake of the great food that comes from its kitchen.

Nearly a quarter of Norwalk's population is Hispanic, and the predominant country of origin for this thriving group of relative newcomers is Colombia. Antojos and several other restaurants in Norwalk cater specifically to the tastes of the Colombian community. It's a cuisine that showcases such Latin American staples as plantains, corn cakes, pork, sausages, and fried eggs atop many dishes.

The interior of Antojos is spare—a long, narrow, wood-paneled space leading to an order window separating the 10 or so dining tables from the kitchen. A chalkboard displays the specials of the day, and the regular menu comes in the form of a printed take-out menu.

Arepas (fried corn pancakes) are a specialty here and are served with *patacones* (fried plantains) along with a variety of meats and sausages, avocado, fried egg, lettuce, tomato, and other garnishes. Antojos's signature dish is an arepa or patacone served with beans, pork belly, chorizo, avocado, and a fried egg. The lunch special is a plate with a little bit of everything at a very affordable price.

One of the most popular dishes is the Papas Rellenas. These baseball-sized potato balls are stuffed with tender, shredded beef then deep fried to crunchy perfection. There's also an array of empanadas stuffed with beef or chicken or both, as well as a Hawaiian version with ham and pineapple.

Left: The lunch special features a little bit of everything.
Right: Try a Colombian soda for a different kind of beverage experience.

Hot dogs and hamburgers are also available and are prepared in various styles, such as Colombian, Hawaiian, and American, each with its own unique garnishes.

The beverage choices at Antojos are quite exotic. There are a few varieties of Colombian sodas as well as the popular "Natural Juices" that come mixed with water or with milk for a creamier texture and flavor. Choose between orange, mango, papaya, strawberry, passion fruit, and blackberry. And for the truly thirsty, there's fresh-squeezed lemonade. No alcohol is served at Antojos, but you won't miss it with this fruit-packed lineup.

115 New Canaan Ave., Norwalk; 203-857-1888
antojoscafe.com

TRAVELER RESTAURANT

Buy a meal, get a free book.

The first things you notice about this roadside eatery are the bright, yellow-tile roof and the large sign stating "Traveler Food and Books." Located off I-84 just south of the Massachusetts border, this combination restaurant and bookstore has one big draw for all travelers: a free book with the purchase of any meal.

This place is a bookworm's dream come true. The knotty-pine dining room and glassed-in porch are filled with shelves and stacks of used books, all there for customers' perusal and taking. There's also a bookstore in the basement, where tens of thousands of used books are for sale.

Current owners Karen and Art Murdock purchased the restaurant from bibliophile Marty Doyle in 1993. Doyle loved books and brought the overflow from his home to the eatery, offering them to customers for free. The Murdocks have kept the tradition going for more than 25 years.

The charming space has the warm look and feel of a reading room, with patrons tucking into meals and wandering around, perusing the shelves and stacks, which also include a broad selection of jigsaw puzzles for sale. The glassed-in porch area is particularly appealing, especially for families and larger groups. Kids love to check out all the offerings, giving road-weary parents a break for a quick meal and a cup of coffee in relative peace.

The Traveler's menu is quite simple, and the offerings are thoughtfully and lovingly prepared by the dozen or so cooks and

The Traveler currently gives away some 200,000 books per year.

Top left: The distinctive, yellow-roofed Traveler Restaurant with its eye-catching sign beckons motorists on I-84.

Above left: Every customer is allowed to take a free book home with them. Book donations are also accepted.

Top middle: Pictures show some of the famous authors who have frequented the Traveler over the years.

Above middle: Feel free to peruse the hundreds of used books on display while enjoying your repast at the Traveler.

Right: A mushroom omelet with marble rye toast is a typical breakfast offering.

servers. The highlight of the breakfast offerings is the three-egg omelete filled with a choice of any two meats, veggies, or cheeses. Toast comes on the side.

There's a surprisingly deep menu of battered and fried seafood, such as haddock, clam strips, shrimp, and sea scallops, all served with fries and coleslaw. The Traveler's sweet potato fries are particularly popular as an appetizer for any meal. The burgers are great, and New England turkey dinner with all the trimmings is the top dinner choice.

But the top reason to patronize this oasis on the interstate is the books, books, and more books available for perusal and for taking or buying. Generations of customers come as kids with their parents. Then as parents themselves, years later, they bring their own progeny to dine and read. May the Murdocks keep this blessed place running for many years to come.

1257 Buckley Hwy., Union; 860-684-4920

ARETHUSA FARM DAIRY

Top-tier dairy from award-winning cows

Dairy doesn't get any better in Connecticut than at Arethusa Farm, a relatively recent upstart in the world of high-end dairy farming. The actual farm got its modern-day start in 1999 when Anthony Yurgaitis and George Malkemus purchased acreage in Litchfield to preserve it as farmland and save it from development. A couple of years later, they began purchasing an all-star lineup of dairy cattle that would, in short order, start bringing in awards from dairy shows nationally and internationally.

One happy offshoot of their wonderful dairy farm resurrection efforts is the amazing dairy store that Arethusa runs in the borough of Bantam, west of downtown Litchfield. Housed in a beautifully restored brick building on Bantam Road that used to be the local firehouse, the Arethusa Farm Dairy treats customers to amazing ice cream, cheeses, fresh milk, and other dairy products made right on the premises. You can view the processing plant through a large window lining the back of the retail space. Thousands of gallons of Arethusa milk are lovingly made into what you find in the store, demonstrating an immediacy that's both comforting and edifying.

The black-and-white motif of the retail space echoes the color scheme of Arethusa's Holstein cows, one of three types of breeds the dairy lovingly cares for on its nearby farm. (The other two are Jersey and Brown Swiss.) Tubs of fresh-churned ice cream in a variety of flavors tempt through glass partitions on the counter. In addition to

On Saturdays in the warmer months, tours of Arethusa Farm are conducted free of charge to the public. Check Arethusa's website in season for details.

Left: Arethusa Farm Dairy store is housed in a beautifully restored former firehouse.

Top middle: Arethusa's ice cream shop on Chapel Street in New Haven.

Above middle: The cheese case is packed with all sorts of award-winning Arethusa cheeses.

Top right: Down on the farm at Arethusa's dairy operation. (Courtesy of Arethusa Farm).

Above right: Arethusa's tastefully appointed ice cream counter.

the standard vanilla, chocolate, and strawberry varieties, there are a myriad of regular and special flavors to choose from, such as sweet cream with chocolate chips, smoked chocolate with sea-salt hazelnut toffee, peppermint, rum raisin, and cranberry almond. Waffle cones are the way to go, and they're generously packed to bursting with any combination of flavors that fit your fancy.

Cheese is made on the premises, including the famous Arethusa Blue, a heady blue cheese modeled on classic farmhouse blues from the British Isles. Other favorites from the copious cheese baskets in the refrigerator cases include Camembert, Tapping Reeve, Europa, and Mt. Tom, named after a famous local peak.

Fresh-churned butter, eggs, milk, and yogurt round out the dairy offerings.

822 Bantam Rd., Bantam; 860-361-6460
arethusafarm.com

SULTAN'S TURKISH RESTAURANT

Have a little belly dancing with your babaganoush and kebabs

With all the fine Italian eateries in Waterbury, Sultan's Turkish Restaurant stands out as a unique and welcome alternative. Positioned right next to busy I-84, this Turkish restaurant is one of the most popular eating spots in the city. And it offers belly-dancing performances on Saturday nights.

Owned by Tannel Atkas, Sultan's opened about 10 years ago in the space previously occupied by another Turkish restaurant (and before that, a Friendly's restaurant). Atkas took Sultan's to a whole new level with a vastly expanded menu, a redecorated dining room, and a Middle Eastern bodega-type grocery adjacent to the restaurant.

The large dining room is done in warm, bright Mediterranean colors of light blue and white, and there are a couple of murals depicting the skyline of Istanbul and the Bosporus. Ottoman tea vessels and other quaint dishware are shelved on the walls next to brightly colored Middle Eastern tapestries.

Turkish food dominates the menu, along with a variety of other Middle Eastern and Mediterranean delicacies. For starters, try the lentil soup made with red lentils and a blend of Turkish seasonings. Most salads are of the Mediterranean variety, loaded with crisp, chopped vegetables and tossed with lemon juice and virgin olive oil. Perhaps the best of the bunch is the Piyaz Salatasi: white beans, romaine lettuce, parsley, onions, and diced tomatoes bathed in a light mixture of olive oil, lemon, and vinegar.

The mixed cold appetizer platter brings together the best of Sultan's classic Middle Eastern dips. Generous portions of hummus,

Top left: The Sultan's Kebab is a potpourri of lamb and vegetables in a flavorful tomato sauce.

Above left: Sultan's dining room is bright and cheerful with murals of Istanbul and the Bosporus.

Above right: The mixed cold appetizer platter provides an array of flavors and textures for slathering on pieces of home-baked bread.

babaganush, *haydari* (yogurt dip), *soslu patlican* (eggplant in tomato sauce), *antep ezme* (chopped tomatoes, onions, garlic, and peppers), and *havoc tarator* (carrot dip) come with slabs of fresh-baked bread. Grilled or fried calamari are great hot appetizers to try.

Kebabs dominate the entrées and come in an array of types. The Doner (thin slabs of seasoned lamb and beef sliced off a vertical spit) is very popular. The Sultan's Kebab features chunks of lamb, onions, bell peppers, thinly sliced eggplant, and zucchini, all covered in a special tomato sauce. On the seafood side, try Levrek (sea bass), which consists of the entire fish expertly grilled.

Check ahead to see if there will be belly dancing or other entertainment on Saturday evenings, the most festive time to visit Sultan's. And be sure to stop by the tiny grocery to pick up Middle Eastern snacks, treats, and ingredients before heading for home.

586 Plank Rd., Waterbury; 203-591-8450
sultansrestaurantct.com

ABBOTT'S LOBSTER IN THE ROUGH

Slow-steamed lobsters in the great outdoors

Situated on the banks of Noank Harbor, Abbott's Lobster in the Rough reigns supreme in the world of Connecticut seafood shacks. From its hot buttered lobster rolls to its slow-steamed lobsters, clams, and mussels to its chowders, chips, and magnificent harborside views, Abbott's should be on every seafood lover's list of must-visits along the Connecticut Shore.

Converted from an old cannery into a lobster shack by Ernie Abbott in 1947, Abbott's is currently under the ownership and management of the Mears family, which has been at the helm since the early 1980s. Dierdre Mears and her daughter, Chelsea, preside over a sprawling operation that features outdoor picnic tables, a small indoor dining area, a dock, an ice cream stand, and a raw bar, all with views of the picturesque harbor.

Start your Abbott's experience with a cup of chowder. There are three kinds: clear-broth clam chowder, creamy New England clam chowder, and shrimp and corn chowder. Lobster bisque is another option. From there, move on to steamed mussels or clams, steamed or chilled shrimp, or the "Abbottizer"—fresh vegetables and fruit served with cheese and crackers.

Lobster is the main show here, and you may opt for a whole steamed lobster or one of Abbott's highly popular lobster rolls. The whole lobster dinner features a slow-steamed lobster along with homemade coleslaw, a bag of potato chips, and a cup of drawn butter. Pick your size—anywhere from 1 1/4 pounds up to a 10-pounder!

Top left: Abbott's famous lobster roll—the sandwich that launches 10,000 SUVs every summer.

Above left: Three generations of Mears family ownership.

Right: Dining on Abbott's harborside dock is a great way to spend a summer evening.

The hot buttered lobster rolls here are legendary and are served several different ways. There's the standard version with a quarter pound of warm, buttered lobster meat served on a somewhat unconventional hamburger bun. The "OMG" version doubles the amount of lobster meat, and the "LOL" features an over-the-top full pound of lobster, enough for at least two or more hungry people. You can also feast on cold lobster, crab, and tuna salad rolls, along with many other offerings.

Abbott's is a BYO establishment, so feel free to bring beer and wine to the party.

117 Pearl St., Noank; 860-536-7719
abbottslobster.com

"Dine in the rough" means you order your food through a window at the front of the shingled shack. Once you pay for your order, you're given a claim number, then you can scout out a place to sit. When your number is called, head inside the shack to pick up your goodies.

A little bit of Budapest in the Hat City

This Hungarian oddity is hidden in a residential, working-class neighborhood of Danbury, attached to a large frame house on a corner lot. It has all the appeal of an Eastern European neighborhood eatery, right down to its family-room look and feel and its heartwarming menu of Hungarian staples, including its namesake goulash. Owner John Aczel presides over this little gem of a restaurant, cooking in the kitchen, tending bar, and chatting to customers throughout the day.

Goulash Place was originally opened in 1977 by Aczel and his late wife, Magda. The couple purchased the storefront next to their home that had housed a Hungarian butcher shop. Initially serving mostly fellow Hungarians in the neighborhood, word spread, causing curious diners to start coming from further afield.

Aczel has kept the menu pretty much the same since opening Goulash Place. By doing so, he can safely lay claim to being the longest standing (and at this point, the only) Hungarian restaurant in the state.

The homemade chicken noodle soup is the best place to start, followed by a crisp, cool cucumber salad. The Special Plate entrée features a bit of everything (except the goulash), including wiener schnitzel, stuffed veal shoulder, roast pork loin, red cabbage, and potatoes, all bathed in a tasty gravy.

The goulash takes center stage here, with the Transylvania goulash being the most popular version: pork simmered in sauerkraut and served with dumplings. The Hungarian goulash is more like a thick meat soup with boiled potatoes and mixed vegetables. One more Hungarian specialty to consider is the

Top left: The interior of Goulash Place is very homey and reminiscent of a quaint European neighborhood eatery.

Above left: The Special Plate features a little bit of everything.

Right: Goulash Place is a charming sight on a residential street in Danbury.

Chicken Paprikas, served with tender, chewy dumplings. Crepe desserts are quite a delightful way to wrap up your lunch or dinner.

It would be a crime to finish your Hungarian feast without some apple or blueberry strudel or, better yet, some palacsinta. These traditional Hungarian crepes are lovingly made by Aczel in his kitchen and come filled with your choice of cottage cheese, apricot, strawberry, chocolate, or chopped nuts. Fresh-brewed coffee is de rigueur with any of these tasty treats.

42 Highland Ave., Danbury; 203-744-1971
goulashplace.com

A one-trick pony that never disappoints

"**N**ever Forget Your Roots" is the motto at this authentic Vietnamese restaurant in East Hartford. It's displayed on the sign above the front door and on the beautifully painted mural on the restaurant's side facing the parking lot. The mural is a depiction of Pho 501 founder Toan Mguyen's early life in Vietnam as well as the important people (and pets) that form his roots and his families in both Asia and America.

Mguyen founded the restaurant in 1992 as a continuation of a restaurant named the Omelette House. He served omelets with baguettes of bread on weekdays and then switched to Vietnamese cuisine on the weekends. Vietnamese restaurants and cuisine were virtually nonexistent in central Connecticut at the time. Customers were initially baffled by the dishes being served, but they took to the broth-and-noodle soup known as pho. Most of the menu was dropped, and pho took center stage.

Today, pho still dominates, and it's what nearly everyone comes here for. There are various types served at different times during the week. The bowls come in small, medium, and large sizes. The basic pho consists of noodles, broth (usually beef), meats or shrimp, onion, cilantro, and scallions. A medium or large bowl is a meal by itself. On weekdays, there are fried chicken wings, spring rolls, and egg rolls as side dishes.

Saturdays feature what is perhaps Pho 501's most famous offering: Bun Bo Hue, a spicy beef broth with beef shank, a few pieces of pork, and Vietnamese-style ham. It's far and away 501's most popular dish and usually sells out by early afternoon. On Sundays, you may get Mi Ga, a pho that consists of chicken broth, al dente egg noodles, and your choice of dark chicken meat or boneless, shredded white chicken.

Top left: Never Forget Your Roots is the motto proudly displayed over the front door of Pho 501.

Above left: Pho with shrimp, noodles, onion, cilantro, and scallions.

Middle: Each order of pho comes with fresh lime, bean sprouts, and cilantro leaves on the side.

Top right: Lean, tender, rare slices of beef along with rich beef broth and all the trimmings make for a warm, satisfying meal in a bowl.

Above right: This beautiful mural on the side of the building tells the story of owner Toan Mguyen's odyssey to America and the early years of Pho 501.

Should you really wish to load up on pho extras, you may (for a slight upcharge) get flank steak, tendon, fatty brisket, oxtail (very popular and flavorful), meatballs, or sliced brisket. The broths simmer on the stovetops continuously throughout the day, evening, and week, guaranteeing consistently excellent flavor and body.

Much of Pho 501's business is carryout; there's even a pho kit of sorts that you can cook up at home. If you'd like to dine in, there are a handful of tables in front of the order counter and in an adjacent room. It's a cozy atmosphere and a great place to tuck into and slurp an excellent bowl of expertly prepared Vietnamese comfort food.

501 Main St. #5, East Hartford; 860-569-3700
pho501.com

Each batch of broth used in 501's phos simmers on the stovetop for 24 hours before being served.

FRANK PEPE'S PIZZA NAPOLETANA

New Haven pizza's Garden of Eden

Regarded by many to have the best pizza in America (if not the world), Frank Pepe's Pizzeria, usually just referred to as "Pepe's," is the gold standard for New Haven-style pizza. Founded in 1925 on New Haven's Wooster Street, Pepe's is the original coal-fired pizza that still uses a coal oven to this day. (There are more than 10 Pepe's locations around the Northeast, but we're going to focus on the original Wooster Street pizzeria.)

Pepe's originated the thin-crust, New Haven-style "apizza" (pronounced *ah-BEETZ*) upon which the pizzeria's reputation is built. Founder Frank's first pizza was a tomato pie—tomatoes with grated pecorino romano cheese, garlic, oregano, and olive oil. It remains one of Pepe's most popular pizzas to this day. The other Pepe's original from the early days is its white clam pizza, made with olive oil, oregano, grated cheese, chopped garlic, and fresh minced littleneck clams. From these starting points, the modern-day Pepe's has blossomed into a generations-old family institution with thin-crust pizzas of every kind.

The Wooster Street restaurant appears much as it did nearly a hundred years ago. The front room is lined with wooden booths, and there's a wooden bar (now a staging area) leading back to the white-tiled, coal-fired oven in the back of the building. The oven, with its numerous long-handled wooden pizza paddles used to maneuver pies around the 600-degree oven, is a sight to behold. It's plainly visible to curious customers and a joy to watch in action. There's another side room of tables, but try to score a booth in the main room in order to take in all the action.

Left: You know you've arrived at pizza nirvana when you see this sign on Wooster Street.

Top middle: The front dining room with the white-tiled pizza oven in full view.

Above middle: Workers using long-handled paddles to maneuver pizzas in the coal-burning oven.

Top right: A pie to go, fresh out of the oven.

Above right: Pepe's custom cardboard boxes, ready for carryout or leftovers.

The menu offers a broad array of pizza toppings, but it's best to stick to those that hew closely to Pepe's Italian roots. For example, try the imported Italian Abruzzo olives, the fresh garlic, the imported Italian anchovies, or the oven-roasted red bell peppers. These toppings deliver the true Pepe's flavor and experience.

With regard to specialty pizzas other than the tomato and white clam pies, there's a spinach, mushroom, and gorgonzola; a Margherita with fresh basil; a veggie special; and a meat-lover's pie.

Locally made Foxon Park soda is the beverage of choice, and there's a modest selection of beer and wine for those so inclined. Oh, and don't forget to start with a Caesar salad. Life always looks brighter after pizza at Pepe's.

157 Wooster St., New Haven; 203-865-5762
pepespizzeria.com

B. F. CLYDE'S CIDER MILL

Cider (and more) made the old-fashioned way

Located a few miles inland from Mystic's famed waterfront, B. F. Clyde's is a genuine steam-powered, wood-press cider mill that's only open from September through early December. It's a must-stop on any leaf-peeping trip through eastern Connecticut and a great destination for families seeking a fun, educational place to take the kids.

The mill started making hard cider in 1881, and Frank and Abby Clyde built the beautiful gingerbread Victorian-style building that forms the centerpiece of the charming mill complex in 1898. They also purchased the steam-driven mill press equipment in the late 1800s—the same equipment used today to extract juice from locally grown apples to make cider and so much more. Clyde's is the only remaining steam-powered cider mill in America, and it's been placed on the National Register of Historic Places.

Wander the grounds to take in the cider press and its truckloads of freshly picked apples. There's also a copiously stocked store in the Victorian house and a charming free tasting room for hard ciders in its own cabin-like building. Demonstrations of the cider mill in action are typically on weekends, but check in advance to find out the schedule during any given week.

Should you wish to sample some of the hard ciders, free tastings are offered in Clyde's Tasting Room. Try such treats as B. F. Clyde's Old Fashioned Hard Cider (the original), Clyde's Cider House blend with cranberries and orange, and Clyde's Spider Cider with spices and natural pumpkin flavoring.

Left: A cup of hot apple cider and a fresh cider donut on an autumn afternoon.

Top middle: A truckload of local apples ready for loading into the cider mill.

Above middle: B. F. Clyde's famous hard cider is for sale in the tasting room.

Right: The old cider mill, where apples are pressed using old, steam-operated equipment.

B. F. Clyde's is a great place to stock up on all your autumn goodies, many of which are made right on the premises and offered for sale in the Victorian house. There is freshly pressed apple cider by the quart, half gallon, and gallon, along with alcoholic hard ciders of various types that have been aged in oak barrels. Homemade apple butter is another popular item, along with fresh-baked cider donuts. Loaves of pumpkin bread and homemade apple pies fly off the shelves throughout the autumn season. There's also plenty of open-air seating at chairs and tables scattered around the grounds.

Plan on spending at least a couple of hours touring the grounds, shopping the store, and enjoying a hot cider and cider donut on the grounds before taking off. Many couples and families have made this an annual pilgrimage, and you'll see why after just one visit.

129 N. Stonington Rd., Old Mystic; 860-536-3354
clydescidermill.com

As much fun as the name implies

Any place with the name "Monkey Farm" is bound to draw bemused attention from prospective diners and passersby, and with good reason. This stalwart watering hole and eatery on Boston Post Road in Old Saybrook looks the part—and serves great food to boot.

Housed in what used to be a roadside inn near the train station, the classic two-story, post-and-beam building from the early 1800s features a glassed-in, year-round, wraparound porch for dining and a dark, cozy interior with tables, a convivial bar, dart boards, a pool table, and more. It serves as an informal meeting place for locals, including elected officials, and it engenders conversation between folks from all walks of life who enter its warm, friendly atmosphere.

The story goes that Harry Corning bought the disused inn, tavern, and eatery in 1968; evicted the mainly older male tenants from the upstairs rooms; and focused on the bar business and a simple menu of sandwiches. The Monkey Farm moniker officially appeared on the building in 1978, though there's no general agreement on where exactly the name came from.

Fast-forward to more recent times: Corning's children have taken over management of the Farm, the kitchen was remodeled in 2006, the menu was expanded, and the establishment's reputation as an eatery of distinction began to spread. The menu is surprisingly varied, starting with basic sandwiches (ham, turkey, roast beef) and amazingly good burgers. Try the half-pounder or go all-in with the 12-ounce burger. They're good, honest burgers, using hand-ground beef that's perfectly grilled.

Fresh seafood comes broiled, fried, or baked and stuffed in a variety of combinations. Ahi tuna is featured as an appetizer in an unusual

Top left: The Monkey Farm sits hard by Route 1 in Old Saybrook, beckoning travelers to stop in for a beverage and some fine food.

Above left: The burgers are massive, juicy, and no-nonsense, a throwback to simpler times.

Top right: The grilled ahi tuna salad with mandarin oranges, tomatoes, craisins, gorgonzola cheese, and avocado.

Above right: The Monkey Farm's interior still has many of its original features from the early 1800s.

nacho-type dish; it also tops a large salad with mandarin oranges, craisins, gorgonzola, and avocado—not what you'd expect from a place called Monkey Farm. Two other food groups to consider: steaks and chops, expertly grilled and served with generous vegetable and potato sides; and delightful, 12-inch personal pizzas, perfect for nibbling while watching the games on the bar's numerous televisions.

Every town should have a place like the Monkey Farm, where locals gather; visitors are welcome; darts, pool, and pinball are played with enthusiasm; and the beer and other libations flow freely. The next time you're passing by the beckoning neon "Monkey Farm" signs outside, pull in, grab a stool or a booth, and soak up the suds and victuals at this Old Saybrook classic.

571 Boston Post Rd., Old Saybrook; 860-388-4866
themonkeyfarmcafe.com

Darts is a popular game here, drawing enthusiasts from around the nation and even from overseas.

FROG ROCK REST STOP

A colorful oasis in Connecticut's Quiet Corner

Eateries don't get much more unique than Frog Rock Rest Stop. This roadside pullover in the verdant woods of Eastford provides a break from driving Route 44 in the summertime.

The namesake rock was first painted and turned into an attraction in 1881 by state legislator Thomas J. Thurber from nearby Putnam. Thurber passed the rock frequently on trips to the state capital and thought it resembled the shape of a squatting frog. The location also became a popular roadside picnic area for many years for people traveling between Hartford and Providence.

A group of Thurber's descendants repainted it in 1997, pledged to maintain Frog Rock in perpetuity, and added a memorial to Thurber on a nearby rock. Several concrete picnic tables were installed and remain to this day.

A subsequent rerouting of Route 44 left Frog Rock further from passing traffic. The State of Connecticut offered the land to neighboring towns, received no offers, and then put the site up for sale. In 2012, local house painter Joe Lernould bought the property and gave the frog a fresh coat of paint.

Since then, Lernould has transformed the pit stop into an oasis that features a small general store, an antique shop, a snack bar, a playground for kids, and a small outdoor stage. There are a bunch of picnic tables scattered around the grounds.

The menu is basic, with offerings such as hot dogs, hamburgers, and grilled cheese. From the deep fryers come whole-belly and strip clams, clam cakes, French fries, onion rings, and mozzarella sticks. There are also hot and cold lobster rolls. Soft-serve ice cream and milkshakes are offered for those seeking something sweet.

Top left: The seasonal food stand offers an amazing variety of foods and snacks.

Above left: This quaint building houses a small general store, an antique shop, and a small outdoor music stage.

Right: The namesake rock, painted in green, froglike splendor, is the rest stop's centerpiece.

This is a great spot for a day trip with the kids, who will get a kick out of the big green frog and enjoy frolicking in the playground and exploring the quaint wooden buildings on the property.

Given its open-air setting, Frog Rock is seasonal, open roughly from May through September. Call ahead before making the trek.

212 Pomfret Rd., Eastford; 860-942-0131

A mid-century diner with Polish pizzazz

The Berlin Turnpike has its fair share of casual eateries, and Makris Diner is one of the best. Housed in a 1951 O'Mahony chrome diner and presided over by charming Polish owner Eva Nowak, the Makris serves up classic diner fare with some fine Polish cuisine on the side.

Step up and into this lovingly restored diner car and grab a stool or a booth in the elongated dining space. Recessed lighting in the curved ceiling casts a warm glow throughout the diner, making you feel instantly at home.

Eva's warm personality is responsible for the steady stream of regulars who stop in to exchange news of the day and enjoy a cup of Makris's specially roasted and brewed coffee. Those who stay for breakfast dine on omelets, a variety of pancakes (including Polish potato pancakes served with applesauce), and various egg breakfasts paired with home fries, toast, bacon, sausage, and ham.

The lunch menu has an impressive lineup of burgers, grinders, and sandwiches, but the dish of choice is the Polish Platter—stuffed cabbage, pierogis, grilled kielbasa, and *kapusta* (Polish sauerkraut). It's this platter that sets Makris apart from most other diners in the state. Stop by and give it a try.

1797 Berlin Trpk., Wethersfield; 860-257-7006
i-love-makris.com

Be sure to check out the original Jerry O'Mahony nameplate, which hangs over the front entrance, lending street cred to the Makris's authenticity as a true mid-century diner.

Top: The Makris Diner, a vintage 1951 Jerry O'Mahony stainless-steel diner in mint condition, sits astride the southbound lanes of the Berlin Turnpike.

Above left: A view of the lengthy Makris interior, lined with vinyl booths and plenty of counter stools.

Above right: Eva Nowak's famous Polish Platter.

Fine grilled meats, Brazilian style

Just down the street from the main campus of Western
Connecticut State University is a nifty Brazilian cafeteria-style
eatery, catering to students and Brazilian transplants alike. It's
a great place to get an introduction to the wonders of Brazilian
cuisine, including some excellent barbecue from Minas's authentic
brick oven barbecue pit.

Originally opened in 1997, Minas was a magnet for Danbury's
growing Brazilian population from the get-go, delivering authentic
Brazilian cuisine in an informal, friendly atmosphere. Others in
the community, including Western Connecticut State students
and faculty, have helped the eatery thrive in its working-class
neighborhood. The two-storefront corner building has had several
different exterior paint jobs over the years, always lending a fresh and
cheerful look.

The most popular part of Minas is its cafeteria-style lineup of
steam tables laden with all sorts of fruit, vegetable, and meat dishes.
Queue up just inside the front door and study the menus on the wall.
Many Brazilian staples are regularly featured, along with a rotating
bunch of specials. Victuals are sold by the pound (along with the
grilled meats), and there are some à la carte items such as empanadas
(beef or cheese), *coxinas* (chicken fritters), and *pao de queijo* (Brazilian
cheesy bread) available at fixed prices, all under $10.

The first steam table offers tempting salads such as collards, garbanzo
beans, cherry tomatoes, beets, and more. Move on to the next tables to
choose from such items as fried plantains, chicken wings, black beans
with sausage and rice, various roasted meats (mostly pork) in delectable
sauces, and even spaghetti with tomato sauce.

Left: A meat handler deftly carving fresh slabs from the pit.

Top middle: Minas Carne, home to the best Brazilian barbecue in western Connecticut.

Above middle: Copious amounts of vegetables and other goodies are offered along with the grilled meats.

Top right: The brick-oven barbecue pit, where all sorts of meats (and pineapple) are slow-roasted to perfection.

Above right: A typical plate of meat, greens, rice, and beans for dining in or to go.

    Leave room on your plate for the star of the show: grilled meats. The barbecue pit is front and center behind the counter, with about 20 skewers of roasting meats at any given time. The skewers are hand-turned, removed from the pit, then expertly carved before you on a large, wooden butcher-block table. Let the carver know which type of meat you prefer, though the grilled beef, a Minas specialty, should be a must-have. It typically comes out a nice, pink, medium-rare. Other grilled meat offerings include chicken breast with bacon, chicken wings, pork tenderloin, beef ribs, and linguiça sausage.

    If you'd prefer a sandwich, there's a short deli counter at the end of the line that will make you a sandwich to your specifications.

36 Osborne St., Danbury; 203-797-9800
minascarne.com

> Grilled whole pineapple is a specialty worth trying from the barbecue pit.

Great vegan cooking paired with a feminist bookstore

Tucked away on a dead-end street in Bridgeport's Black Rock neighborhood is the famed Bloodroot Vegetarian Restaurant and Feminist Bookstore. This labor of love is housed in a quaint, cedar-shingled house with a view of tidal Burr Creek. It's a beautiful spot in a quiet corner of Connecticut's largest city, and if you're a vegetarian or vegan (and even if you're not), this place should be on your short list of places to dine.

Founded in 1977 by four women as part of a feminist collective, it morphed into a vegetarian restaurant and feminist bookstore helmed by partners Selma Miriam and Noel Furie. They named it Bloodroot after a Connecticut wildflower, and they still run it to this day.

Selma sits at her desk by the entrance, armed with an order pad. Across from her is a window-like opening into the kitchen where Noel and her cook staff are at work. A chalkboard menu hangs above the opening. Study the menu, then place your order with Selma. When your food is ready, it will be presented on a tray by the kitchen window for easy pickup. There is no table service, and you're expected to bus your dishes when you're finished.

Bloodroot's dining room is small, dimly lit, and filled with antique wooden tables and chairs. It's a warm and charming setting made even more intriguing by the dozens of framed photos of feminist icons lining the walls. The bookstore is in a back room just off the kitchen.

Should the weather be fair, consider dining on Bloodroot's rustic patio with lovely plantings and a view of Burr Creek.

Top left: Bloodroot's weathered exterior, looking much as it did when it opened more than 40 years ago.

Above left: A fresh, crisp, seasonal Bloodroot salad.

Top right: Ginger carrot soup and fresh-baked bread.

Above right: Bloodroot's airy patio is a great place to dine in fair-weather months.

Right: Patty Shea, Noel Furie, and Selma Miriam. (Courtesy of Bloodroot.)

The cooking at Bloodroot rivals that of any vegan/vegetarian fare you'll find anywhere. The food is made with love and experience, it's all prepared from scratch, and the menu changes with the seasons. Soups include such offerings as spicy gingered carrot; chickpea, carrot, and potato with tomato; and gazpacho. The mushroom walnut paté is a great appetizer, as is the vegan cheese taster. There are several seasonal salad offerings, such as marinated tofu and Chinese cabbage, along with the regulars shredded beet, carrots, turnip, and avocado.

Jamaican jerk "chicken," an entrée creation of one of Noel's stalwart staff, is a perennial favorite here along with such seasonal specials as Vietnamese summer rolls, Mexican mole "chicken," and chilled Szechuan noodles. Fresh-baked daily bread and amazing desserts, including vegan ice cream, round out the offerings.

85 Ferris St., Bridgeport; 203-576-9168
bloodroot.com

GRANO ARSO

Fresh pasta made daily with local grains

Ascant two years after opening in late 2017, Grano Arso in Chester was named the best restaurant in the state by the Connecticut Restaurant Association. Few would argue with the choice, as this contemporary Italian restaurant steeped in Old World traditions breaks many molds and turns out consistently outstanding cuisine.

The husband-and-wife team of Joel and Lani Gargano work in perfect harmony to create a one-of-a-kind dining experience that takes farm-to-table to a new level of excellence. Joel runs the kitchen and also personally delivers entrées to tables in the beautifully appointed dining room in an old bank building on Chester's main thoroughfare. He's happy to chat with customers as he moves from kitchen to tables, serving as head chef and occasional food runner.

Lani is of Asian descent, and she runs the restaurant's front end, catering to customers' every whim while also spending time behind the handsome bar and in the kitchen to help out when needed. She's responsible for the beautiful interior design of the main dining and special events rooms.

One reason for Grano Arso's unique and rapid success is its delectable pasta and bread made from home-milled flour derived from grains grown throughout New England. Chef Joel toasts the grains in his kitchen after milling, giving them a coarse, smoky texture and flavor. Each meal starts with a slice of home-baked bread and sweet, lightly churned butter, a teaser that hints at the wonderful surprises to come.

The menu changes seasonally and proceeds with a variety of small plates, such as roasted Castelvetrano olives, an amazing Crostino with whipped gorgonzola, a generous helping of steamed mussels marinara,

Top left: Rigatoni Bolognese, a regular feature on Grano Arso's menu.

Above left: Grano Arso is housed in a beautiful 1902 bank building on Chester's main thoroughfare.

Middle: The eggplant al forno appetizer.

Right: One of Grano Arso's nicely decorated dining rooms.

and roasted carrots with miso vinaigrette, ricotta, pistachio, and hot honey. All this sets the stage for the pasta and large plates to follow.

Chef Joel and his team make all their own fresh pasta daily using painstaking, Old-World methods. The end result is a wide variety of dishes that take advantage of the local bounty, depending on the season. One stalwart on the menu is the rigatoni Bolognese, featuring a beef ragu, parmigiano Reggiano, and whole basil leaves as a garnish. There's always a special spaghetti dish that frequently features fresh clams, mussels, scallops, and toasted bread crumbs. This is pasta like you've never had before.

6 Main St., Chester; 860-322-3143
granoct.com

Co-owner Lani Gargano occasionally takes over in the kitchen when Grano Arso goes into pop-up Vietnamese food mode. It's a great added dimension to the Grano Arso experience.

REIN'S NEW YORK—STYLE DELI

A bit of Brooklyn in the Hartford 'burbs

"Food that feeds the soul and warms the heart."

Like a Jewish oasis on I-84 between Gotham and Beantown, Rein's Deli has all the trappings of an authentic New York deli. From its order counter stocked with smoked and pickled fish, deli meats, potato pancakes, and traditional Jewish salads and spreads, to its voluminous dining rooms complete with an eight-foot-tall scale model of the Statue of Liberty, this place makes all New Yorkers, native or otherwise, feel right at home.

Like all good Jewish delis, Rein's has a menu that goes on for pages and pages with a stupefying array of breakfast, lunch, dinner, dessert, and beverage options that will leave your head spinning. Choose from such deli standards as corned beef or pastrami Rueben/Rachael sandwiches, borscht, cheese blintzes, roasted brisket, homemade *ruggalach* (cream cheese and butter pastry), and more. Wash down your meal with an authentic egg cream, and you'll think you're on the Lower East Side.

Hebrew National meats are served here, and all sandwiches are custom-made and hand-sliced by expert deli counter workers. Ten different types of bagels are baked daily on the premises, along with rye bread, pumpernickel, bialys, and various cakes and cookies. Rein's New York cheesecake is particularly popular with customers.

The dining area is partitioned into several sections, each one named after a different New York City borough. In the back of the dining room is the whimsically named "Way-Off Broadway Lounge," where one can grab a stool at the bar and enjoy a drink or two. An army of

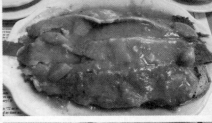

Left: The crazy, crowded deli counter offers all sorts of Jewish delicacies and prepared foods. It's also where you can order amazing sandwiches to go.

Top right: The hot open roasted brisket with potatoes and coleslaw is one of dozens of sandwiches and entrées on Rein's voluminous menu.

Above right: Smoked whitefish is always on hand at the deli counter.

servers and bussers swarm over the dining areas at all times, making sure customers have everything they need.

Rein's is the brainchild of Bob Rein, who founded the deli in 1972 along with his wife and his brother. Frustrated that he couldn't find a good corned beef sandwich in northern Connecticut, he decided to open his own place, succeeding beyond his wildest dreams. The Rein family still owns and runs the deli, and its popularity hasn't waned over the years, a testament to great food, superior service, and an undying commitment to making customers feel like they're at home.

435 Hartford Tpke., Vernon; 860-875-1344
reinsdeli.com

Whether or not you're an M.O.T. ("member of the tribe"), you'll find plenty to like here in the way of authentic Jewish cuisine and hospitality. *L'chaim!*

ATLANTIC SEAFOOD MARKET

The finest, freshest seafood on the shoreline

There are plenty of places to get fresh seafood on the Connecticut Shore, and Atlantic Seafood is the best of the bunch. This little jewel takes its seafood very seriously.

The whitewashed roadside stand on Boston Post Road with its bright, red awning is chock-full of seafood surprises—from its award-winning cold lobster roll to its in-house, fresh-cut fish fillets, to wonderful seasonal specials on such local favorites as shad, blackfish, smelts, soft-shell crab, and Nantucket bay scallops.

Lisa Friedman has been at the helm of Atlantic Seafood for the past 15 years. She was shopping around for a business that was closer to home during her child-rearing years, and she also wanted to get out of her careers in real estate and furniture. She had no background in retail seafood when she purchased the humble business. In fact, the closest she and her husband had come to the seafood trade was catching mako sharks on their boat and selling them to fishermen in Montauk, New York, to help pay the cost of gas to run their boat while sportfishing.

Friedman keeps her seafood cases and lobster tank filled with all sorts of tempting delights. Fresh-cut tuna, salmon, cod, halibut, haddock, and more are year-round offerings in the fresh fish case, along with steamer and littleneck clams, gulf shrimp, and massive sea scallops. The live lobsters come from Maine and are of the hardshell variety, meaning they're packed with lobster meat and perfect for boiling or steaming.

Friedman's tireless efforts are augmented by partner and resident chef Jerry Doran, a Culinary Institute of America–trained seafood specialist. Guided by the philosophy that "less is more," Doran finds joy in creating an array of simple dishes and prepared foods. Daily

Top left: An oasis of seafood goodies on Boston Post Road in Old Saybrook.

Above left: There's an abundance of fresh and packaged seafood choices along with gourmet specialty foods and spices.

Right: The fresh seafood cases are packed with fish and shellfish from around the world.

offerings include cod cakes, lobster ravioli, salmon cakes, tuna cakes, chowders, bisques, Carolina coleslaw, and dill shrimp salad.

This is the place to come for the freshest, best seafood on the Connecticut Shore.

1400 Boston Post Rd., Old Saybrook; 860-388-4527
atlanticseafoodmarket.com

A burger/hot dog/ice cream shack with gourmet flair

US Route 7 has its fair share of drive-in food stands as it winds its way through western Connecticut, and Heibeck's in Wilton may be the best of the bunch. Housed in a couple of low-slung buildings on the west side of the road, backed by a shaded patio, and flanked on one side by a pretty little picnic area, it's a great place to stop for top-notch sandwiches, specials, and small batch ice cream.

This alluring roadside attraction celebrates its 90th anniversary in 2021. Currently owned by a mother-and-son team directly related to the founders, the stand has remained under Heibeck family ownership, except for a 30-year period from the late 1900s to the early 2010s. Son, Skylar, runs the business with his mom, Barbara, who makes sauces from scratch every morning.

One look at the menu boards suspended over the order windows tells you this is no ordinary roadside stand. Heibeck's has carefully honed its offerings over the years, keeping a keen eye on local culinary tastes and trends. The core of the menu remains the superb hot dogs and hamburgers. On the burger side, there are numerous choices, including a couple of veggie/vegan ones. The best picks are the Heibeck Burger (cheese, lettuce, tomato, pickles, and a spicy thousand-island-based Heibeck sauce) and the Cowboy Burger (pepper jack cheese, coleslaw, bacon, barbecue sauce, and frizzled onions). Exotic homemade sauces include chipotle mayo, spicy relish, avocado salsa, and cilantro crema.

As for hot dogs, there are some 10 varieties, the best of which is the chili dog, bathed in Heibeck's famous homemade chili. (Try to come on Tuesdays, when hot dogs are 2-for-1, an amazing deal.) The dogs are Hebrew National and are grilled to crispy perfection.

Left: There's an amazing variety of cones and sundaes, with generous amounts of toppings available at the ice cream window.

Middle: The crew of Heibeck's multi-hued main shack takes your food and ice cream orders and prepares them in back, skillfully and efficiently.

Right: Heibeck's features a "two-fer" on hot dogs each Tuesday. A chili dog is on the left and the "Heibeck" is on the right.

And there's so much more to explore here. Take the tacos: bang-bang shrimp, vegetarian beet, buffalo chicken, and crispy cod are just a few of the choices. Then there's the seafood, with the hot lobster roll sauteed in a wine-butter sauce, fried shrimp, clam strips, and fish-and-chips. Daily specials often include Brussels sprouts, done in such fanciful ways as honey Dijon and spicy Hawaiian.

Stroll into the breezeway between the two Heibeck's buildings to place your order for ice cream. Of the 16-plus flavors, Trash Can is one of the most popular—vanilla ice cream with cookie dough, brownies, heath bar, M&M's, caramel, and fudge.

With this and so much more going on at Heibeck's, it's best to plan more than one trip here, to get the full essence of this classic roadside spot.

951 Danbury Rd., Wilton; 203-917-9313
heibecksstand.com

The stand first opened in 1931 and has experienced many changes over the years, yet it's still owned by a Heibeck—Barbara—and her son, Skylar Smith.

BILL'S SEAFOOD

Deep-fried fun on the Connecticut Shore

Sitting in the shadow of Westbrook's famous "Singing Bridge" on Boston Post Road, Bill's Seafood is a legendary shack with a long history of serving up some of the tastiest, most distinctive seafood on the eastern Connecticut shoreline.

Established in 1950 as an ice cream stand on the banks of the Patchogue River, the small shack morphed into a hot dog stand and then a clam shack known as Del's Fish and Chips before hitting its stride as Bill's under current owner Robert "Butch" Claffey.

Bill's Seafood exudes an "anything goes" feel, with its sun-drenched deck astride the river, its oval-shaped bar in the center of the restaurant, and its freewheeling outdoor lounge area that boasts live music many summer nights. (Jazz bands play indoors in winter.)

The clientele is from all over and includes boaters from the nearby marinas, bikers who park their machines in the crushed-shell parking lot, and families that have been coming for years to enjoy some of the best seafood around. In the middle of summer, the license plates in the parking lot pay testament to the fact that folks come from hundreds of miles away to enjoy an afternoon or evening at this seafood shack and watering hole where people of every stripe seem to mingle just fine.

For starters, try the homemade clam chowder, which comes in the traditional creamy style or clear-broth Rhode Island version. The fried calamari is served straight out of the deep fryer and is accompanied by a cup of marinara sauce. There's also the Point Judith (Rhode Island) version, spiced up with jalapenos, olives, and garlic for the more adventurous. Clams casino, Maryland blue crab cakes, and fragrant, toasty garlic bread with marinara sauce round out the best of the beginners.

Top left: Bill's large outdoor deck is a great spot for summertime fun.

Above left: A basketful of deep-fried clam strips.

Top right: Steamed mussels with garlic bread is a great appetizer.

Above right: Be sure to check out the ice cream shop and gift store next to the seafood shack.

Deep-fried seafood is the most popular main course here, followed closely by Bill's famous hot buttered lobster roll. The deep-fried goodies come in the form of platters (with fries and slaw), rolls (clams, clam strips, oysters, scallops, or shrimp tucked into split-top buns), and Bill's fish-and-chips.

An Ashley's and Gifford's ice cream stand has sprouted in the parking lot for those seeking something sweet after a hot afternoon on Bill's riverside deck. The stand also houses a gift shop. All this and more can be found next to the steel-grated "singing bridge" that gives this seafood mecca a harmonious hum every time a vehicle crosses.

548 Boston Post Rd., Westbrook; 860-399-7224
billsseafood.com

LAKESIDE DINER

Homemade donuts and a placid, duck-filled pond

Lakeside Diner is an old-school eatery in the shadow of the Merritt Parkway, on Long Ridge Road just off southbound exit 34 in northern Stamford. The diner, housed in a modest, whitewashed cinderblock building with red trim, has been serving up belly-filling diner food since the 1950s, and they're particularly renowned for their homemade donuts and extensive pancake offerings.

The diner first opened in a trailer in the early 1950s, but soon after moved into its current home by Holts Ice Pond. It's a bucolic setting, with trees overhanging the water and ducks and other waterfowl frequently paddling about. Current owner Jane Agostino and her husband Dominick bought the Lakeside in 1987, and she has poured her heart and soul into the place ever since.

When you step inside, you step back several decades, as very little has changed here since the diner's inception. There's a counter with a half dozen of the original stools. Hanging over the counter is a blackboard thick with the day's offerings and specials. The Lakeside is particularly known for its breakfasts, which are served all day until closing time (usually around 3 p.m.). The walls are covered with memorabilia in the form of photos and nostalgic kitsch from the diner's days gone by.

But the real beauty of the place is the floor-to-ceiling windows overlooking the pond. Try and grab one of the few tables next to the glass and prepare to be mesmerized by the tranquil scene. In addition

> The most popular pancake dish is the Red, White, and Blue—flapjacks topped with strawberries, bananas, and blueberries.

Left: Try and score a table overlooking the placid pond in back of the diner.

Top middle: The Lakeside's friendly counter, with its original stools.

Top right: A plate of Lakeside Diner's highly touted homemade donuts.

Above right: Lakeside's grilled pastrami sandwich is thick with cured meat, tomatoes, and cheese.

to the pondside indoor tables, there are several picnic-type tables outside for dining and coffee sipping in fair weather. It's hard to believe that the four-lane parkway is less than 100 feet away.

As mentioned, the donuts and pancakes are front and center, and with good reason. The cinnamon-sugar donuts are made fresh daily. Locals stop in for bags and boxes of them all morning long. Piles of fresh-baked donuts are also usually under glass on the counter. The pancakes are of the thin and light variety and are actually fine with just a little butter and syrup.

Omelets are also popular, with about a dozen different types. Though there's a modest selection of lunchtime burgers and other sandwiches, breakfast is definitely the way to go.

1050 Long Ridge Rd., Stamford; 203-322-2252

Pick your own seasonally or shop the store year-round.

There's something about going into an orchard and picking your own fruit that really can't be beat in terms of freshness and fun on a warm summer or autumn day. Bishop's Orchards has been offering such outings—and much more—for decades in the soft rolling hills of Guilford.

The establishment was founded as a general-purpose farm in 1871 by Walter Goodrich Bishop. The Bishop family, which still owns the farm and orchards, opened their first commercial orchard in 1909, and they haven't looked back. Currently under the sixth generation of Bishop family management (with the seventh generation starting to help out), the orchards, farm store, and related operations employ some 60 year-round employees, supplemented by as many as 175 during harvest seasons. It's a surprisingly large agricultural operation for a Connecticut shoreline town.

Bishop's main year-round attraction is its large, white, barnlike retail store on Route 1 a mile or so west of the Guilford green. This gargantuan produce market and more stocks all sorts of seasonal fresh fruits and vegetables, many of them from Bishop's own 300 acres of orchards and vegetable gardens. This is the place to come for the freshest produce on the shoreline. The wood-paneled interior is warm, inviting, and always well stocked with everything from apples, strawberries, blueberries, and raspberries to fresh-baked pies, bread, apple cider donuts, cookies, muffins, cheeses, and more.

In addition to all the fresh produce and baked goods, there are lots of prepared foods such as jellies, jams, homemade soups, cold cuts, wraps, sandwiches, side dishes, and even select meats from a meat counter. Crock-pot meals and grill meals are another specialty, found in the freezer section, ready to take home and heat up for hearty

Top left: It's hard to miss this inviting sign on Route 1 west of downtown Guilford.

Above left: Bishop's makes its own apple cider and apple cider donuts (and holes) year-round.

Top middle: The produce section in the market is a fruit- and vegetable-lover's dream come true.

Above middle: Stop by and sample some of Bishop's many homegrown fruit wines.

Right: Some free sustenance while you shop.

family-style dinners. There's even a winery that offers tastings, tours, and a nice selection of homemade wines and hard ciders.

Perhaps the most popular and best-known activity at Bishop's is picking your own fruits and vegetables from the orchards in season. Strawberries, blueberries, peaches, and pears are ripe for picking in the summer months. Raspberries, apples, and pumpkins may be harvested by hand in the fall. Families with children of all ages make annual pilgrimages to the orchards to pick fresh produce and take it home for eating, canning, or preserving. It's a great way to spend a sunny day in one of the last true working farms on the Connecticut Shore.

1355 Boston Post Rd., Guilford; 203-453-2338
bishopsorchards.com

Apple cider is pressed at Bishop's own cider mill year-round except for the summer months.

HARRY'S PLACE

Burgers, dogs, and cones for 100 years and counting

You'll know that spring has arrived in Colchester when Harry's Place raises its wooden shutters and starts cooking burgers and dogs for their legions of local fans. This venerable drive-in celebrated its 100th anniversary in 2020, and it's poised to keep cranking out its famous road food for many years to come.

Founded by Harry Schmuckler, Harry's has been owned successively by family members and longtime employees. The brother-and-sister team of John and Suzanne Garet currently own and run the stand with the help of family members and many longtime employees.

Harry's has long been famous for their meaty burgers, which come in four-ounce patties or half-pound "stackers." Served on a fluffy bun with your choice of more than 10 toppings, the burgers can be meals unto themselves. But don't deprive yourself of one of more than half a dozen types of French fries, which come dressed with your choice of cheese, bacon, chili, or all of the above.

Hot dogs play a strong second fiddle to the burgers, with many of the same toppings found on the fries. There's also a small selection of fried seafood. Ice cream by the cup or cone round out the culinary experience at this one-of-a-kind historic roadside stand.

104 Broadway St., Colchester; 860-537-2410
harrysplaceburgers.com

Top: Harry's Place, with its signature whitewashed shack and top-suspended wooden counter shutters.

Middle: A couple of Harry's famous burgers, one plain and one with the works.

Bottom: Clam strips and fries make for a nice meal on a summer day.

Home of the world-famous "winged" cheeseburger

Home of the Bernice Original "winged" cheeseburger, Shady Glen has single-handedly put Manchester on the American culinary map. This roadside dairy stand and 1950s-style casual food joint has been feeding locals for around 70 years through three generations of family ownership. The ice cream creations are divine and rival the famed cheeseburger in popularity. It's well worth a special trip from anywhere in the state to experience this warm and wonderful institution.

Back in 1946, John and Bernice Rieg wanted to expand their dairy farm into the ice cream–making business and did so with assistance from the nearby UConn agricultural school. Soon they were churning out top-quality ice cream, which they sold through their nascent dairy store near the town border with Bolton. To encourage year-round patronage, the Riegs added a small line of sandwiches, and, in 1949, Bernice came up with her winged cheeseburger. Cheese slices overlap the burgers on the griddle, then are cooked until the cheese corners turn crisp and curl, resembling wings. This distinctive approach has garnered national attention and a legion of fans from far and wide.

When you enter the restaurant, it's immediately apparent that you've stepped back in time. Yellow-striped wallpaper, recessed lighting, white-aproned waitresses, and bow-tied grill cooks hearken back to the 1950s—but not in a calculated, marketing-type way. This place is the real deal, as if preserved in amber, and the food is as genuine as the decor.

In addition to the winged cheeseburger, there are grilled frankfurters, grilled ham and cheese, tuna salad, egg salad, fries, onion rings, coleslaw, and more, including various platters of

Left: A chocolate sundae is a must-have before, during, or after any meal at Shady Glen.

Top middle: The bow-tied, white-shirted crew manning Shady Glen's busy grill area keep things moving throughout the day.

Above middle: The Glen's world-famous, award-winning winged cheeseburger. Seeing is believing.

Right: Shady Glen serves up good, wholesome food (and plenty of ice cream) year-round.

deep-fried seafood. There's also a short breakfast menu, including pancakes, omelets, eggs, French toast, and home fries.

It's de rigueur to have a homemade milkshake with your burger, dog, or sandwich. Made from scratch and served from tall, stainless-steel mixing receptacles, these shakes don't disappoint. In addition to the standard chocolate and vanilla, Shady Glen's shakes come in more than two dozen ice cream flavors.

For dessert, choose from cones, and cups made from Shady Glen's home-churned ice creams. Consider grabbing a pint or half-gallon of Shady Glen's amazing homemade ice cream from the coolers up front to take home before you leave.

840 Middle Trpk. E., Manchester; 860-649-4245

Chocolate-based sundaes are the most popular, and there are great seasonal choices, such as Melba peach in the spring and pumpkin in the fall.

Haute French cuisine in a historic New Haven landmark

A world-class French brasserie housed in a landmark brick-and-stone building in downtown New Haven is a great recipe for one of the best, most distinctive restaurants in the state. Union League Cafe has been wowing diners since it was founded a couple of decades ago by Jean Pierre Vuillermet. It's currently helmed in the kitchen by Vuillermet's protegee and executive chef Guillaume Traversaz.

A diminutive green neon sign on Chapel Street indicates the location of the café, which is housed in the historic Sherman Building, named after its first occupant, a signer of the Declaration of Independence, the Articles of Confederation, and the US Constitution. Walk through the front door and up a short flight of stairs, where you'll be greeted by a gracious maître d', who will seat you (reservations are almost always essential).

The dining room is a work of art, with its high ceilings, arched windows framed in dark wood, and centerpiece fireplace, always flickering and bringing a warm glow to the entire enterprise. Marble columns accentuate the wood and the hearth, and wooden-arched doorways lead to smaller, more private dining rooms. It's a lovely setting for a romantic dinner or a convivial gathering of family, friends, or business associates.

Seafood is a strong suit at Union League, starting with their raw bar, which offers meaty shrimp with cocktail sauce, raw littleneck clams served with mignonette sauce, and a selection of oysters that changes almost daily. The house-smoked salmon comes thin sliced and is served with pickled red onions, potato blinis, and dill cream. Caviar and white sturgeon are offered in very small (and understandably pricey) quantities, perfect for a special occasion.

Top left: Duck confit with a crispy potato galette and watercress salad is a popular appetizer.

Above left: The green neon sign indicating you've arrived at one of the best restaurants in the state.

Middle: The Union League's tastefully appointed dining room is a beautifully preserved step back in history.

Right: The central fireplace brings a warm glow and homey feel to any meal at Union League.

There's more seafood in the form of appetizers, such as steamed mussels and grilled octopus. Soup offerings change seasonally, and escargot and foie gras serve as reminders that this is, in fact, a brasserie.

The entrées feature such innovative dishes as lobster risotto, seared organic salmon, braised short ribs, and a nice half-pound Black Angus filet with a bordelaise sauce.

France runs the table on the dessert menu, with such offerings as Paris-Brest, a house-made pastry with hazelnut praline mousse, chocolate *dremeuz*, and a caramel sauce. The soufflé du jour is always a pleasant surprise, and crème brulée is infused with pistachio.

With a wine cellar that is virtually unrivaled in the city or state, Union League Cafe stands head and shoulders above virtually all restaurants in Connecticut and is certainly worth a special visit any time of year.

1032 Chapel St., New Haven; 203-562-4299
unionleaguecafe.com

Hot dogs boiled in oil and crisped up on the griddle. Don't forget the pepper relish.

Connecticut has carved out quite a reputation as a hot dog mecca, with a wide variety of wiener styles and eateries that appeal to tube steak aficionados everywhere. Blackie's is one of those unique hot dog emporiums, architecturally and culinarily. It's also been around for a long time.

The Blackman family started selling hot dogs out of their gas station on the Cheshire-Waterbury town line in 1928. Their homemade pepper relish was an instant hit and remains the most popular condiment to this day. Burgers and chips were added to the menu, and little else. The gas pumps are gone, as founder Art Blackman (whose nickname was" Blackie") found that the roadside family business was selling more hot dogs than petrol.

The original Blackie's burned down in 1945, and it was replaced with the current twin-towered, barnlike structure, which sports a couple of large neon Blackie's signs. There are two garage doors in the middle of the facade that are rolled up in the warmer months to let in the breeze. A long counter with stools is front and center inside, flanked by small, tabled dining areas in the towered sections. The atmosphere is cramped and convivial, and the knotty pine walls are covered with Blackie's press clippings and memorabilia.

What makes Blackie's hot dogs so special? First, it's the cooking method. The wieners are boiled in cooking oil until the skin casings split. Dogs may additionally be charred on the griddle upon

> The most noteworthy thing about Blackie's is its homemade hot pepper relish.

Left: Tell the counter help how many hot dogs you want, and then stand back and watch the magic.

Top middle: Blackie's, back in the day when it pumped gas as well as served up hot dogs. (Courtesy of Blackie's.)

Above middle: Blackie's dogs are boiled in oil until the casings split open.

Right: Blackie's ancient neon sign atop its barnlike facade.

request. All Blackie's hamburgers and cheeseburgers are cooked to medium doneness.

The Blackmans came up with the recipe for their hot pepper relish back when they first opened, and they've been serving it ever since. To this day, the family makes a huge batch once a year from their secret recipe. You may also buy a jar of the famous condiment to enjoy at home.

Ordering at Blackie's is simple. Tell the counter help how many hot dogs you want, using only the number desired. Bark out "Two!," "Three!," "Seven!," or whatever quantity you want, and a few minutes later, you'll be handed that many unadorned dogs. (Throw in "Well done!" if you also want them charred on the griddle.) Dress them up with the pepper relish or spicy mustard from one of the countertop condiment boxes and settle in for one of the best hot dogs in the state.

2200 Waterbury Rd., Cheshire; 203-699-1819
blackieshotdogs.com

WILLIMANTIC BREWING COMPANY

The King Kong of Connecticut microbreweries

In a state where a new microbrewery seems to open every week, Willimantic Brewing Company stands as Connecticut's oldest, largest, and perhaps best. Housed in a gorgeous limestone building, "Willibrew," as the brewpub is affectionately known to locals, took over the cavernous former US post office building in 1997 and commenced brewing beers almost immediately. The brewery and its companion restaurant are the undisputed anchors to the vibrant downtown scene in this town that is also home to Eastern Connecticut State University.

Owner and founder David Wollner had a couple of other brewpub restaurants on Willimantic's Main Street before making the big leap to the post office building. There are many reminders of the old post-office days: The pub area, with its 60-foot-long mahogany bar, sits in the former post office lobby. The old back workroom has been converted into a lovely, lofty dining room with 20-foot-high ceilings and nostalgic, whimsical art and dozens of beer tap handles gracing the walls. And there's additional outdoor seating in season with a nice view of Main Street. In short, it's a perfect setting for good food and great beer.

Starting with the beer, Willibrew makes more than a dozen of its own on the premises. Its seven-barrel brewery in and around the main dining room is constantly cooking batches of every type of brew you can imagine. There are blonde, amber, and dark ales; various India Pale Ales (IPAs); stouts; a wide variety of German-style beers; and their famous Willibrew B.A. Willi Oude Whammer (W.o.W.), which packs a whopping 11.3 percent alcohol content. Come back often, as Willibrew is always coming up with new beers for aficionados to try.

Top left: Willibrew's three-bean chili comes loaded with meat, beans, and a tangy, tart tomato sauce.

Above left: Hundreds of tap handles grace the walls throughout Willibrew, a testament to the reverence the place has for craft brewing.

Middle: The high-ceilinged main dining room is filled with whimsical, nostalgic art, some of it reflecting Willimantic's colorful past.

Right: The 60-foot-long mahogany bar occupies what used to be the post office's lobby.

W.B.C. also supports other fine microbrews from around the state and the New England region—such favorites as Allagash White Ale from Portland, Maine; Fat Orange Cat Brew from East Hampton, Connecticut; and New England Cider from Wallingford. One glance at the taps behind the bar reveals the astonishing number of brews available.

On the food front, be sure to try Willibrew's award-winning nachos, a massive plate of chips, beans, cheese, and so much more. The three-bean chili is another popular opener. WBC Steak Poutine features medium-rare garlic sirloin steak, fries, and cheddar-Jack cheese smothered in beer gravy. The Stonington Sausage Platter is a good accompaniment to a pint or two, and sandwiches and wraps of every type abound.

967 Main St., Willimantic; 860-423-6777
willimanticbrewingcompany.com

The former postmaster's office serves as a high-ceilinged dining room for private parties.

BLACK DUCK CAFE

Speedboat nostalgia and good eats on an old barge in the river

If you want to get down and dirty in toney Westport, the Black Duck Cafe is probably your best bet for good, old-fashioned, burger 'n' barroom fun. Sitting atop an ancient barge in the Saugatuck River that bobs in the shadow of an I-95 span above, this hideaway is the perfect spot for a burger and a brew. Owner Peter Aitken is a daredevil powerboat racer-turned-restaurateur, and there's plenty of memorabilia around the place documenting his time on the water.

Climb aboard, grab a stool at the bar, or commandeer a table in the tiny dining room or (weather permitting) one on the outdoor deck. This is a very convivial place, with bankers and brokers mixing it up with bikers and bikini-clad townies, fresh off pleasure craft parked outside.

Burgers are the stars of the Black Duck's menu, with several varieties to choose from. There are burgers stuffed with cheddar, bleu, or brie cheese oozing out with the first bite. There's also the Black Duck Burger, smothered in sauteed bell peppers, onions, and mushrooms. You can't go wrong with any of them.

The limited seafood menu is also popular, especially the fried clam strips, hot buttered lobster rolls, and the clams casino appetizer.

605 Riverside Ave., Westport; 203-227-7978
blackduckwestport.com

Top left: The speedboat motif is big at the Black Duck Cafe.

Above left: The Black Duck's lobster roll platter.

Right: The Black Duck's outdoor deck on the Saugatuck River in the shade of I-95.

Black Duck owner Pete Aitken won the national and world powerboat championships in 1983 and has been inducted into the National Powerboat Association Hall of Fame.

The "other" Wooster Street pizza place (and Frank Sinatra's favorite)

Anchoring one end of legendary Wooster Street in a narrow, storefront brick building, Sally's Apizza is a must-stop for any serious connoisseur of legendary New Haven–style pizza.

Sally's has been owned or run by the Consiglio family since 1938, when Filomena Consiglio (sister of Frank Pepe) bought the restaurant for $500. Filomena's son Sal (aka "Sally") ran the restaurant along with his wife, Flo, and his brother Tony until 1989, using the signature pizza recipes developed by Filomena and Sal. The Consiglios owned Sally's until 2017 when they sold to new owners, but Sal and Flo's sons Bobby and Ricky have stayed on, continuing to run the restaurant.

The modest dining room at Sally's is pretty much the same as it has been for decades. It's a long, narrow space leading to the multicolored, coal-fired brick oven in the back. The walls are lined with booths and tables as well as lots of great photos and newspaper clippings chronicling Sally's storied history. Frank Sinatra was a lifelong fan of Sally's. Whenever he was performing in New York City, he would send someone from his entourage to pick up some Sally's pies and bring them to him for an after-concert meal.

The menu at Sally's is simple and straightforward, and you can't really go wrong no matter what type of pizza you order. It might be best to start with the basics: Sally's famed classic plain pie—crust, grated parmesan cheese, and tomato sauce. Though it may sound pedestrian, it's one of Sally's most popular pies and solid proof that simple things are often the best.

From there, move on to one of Sally's specialty pies. The white fresh tomato pie has tomato, mozzarella, and basil for toppings.

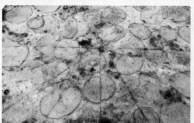

Left: Sally's ancient coal-fired oven has been in service for decades and keeps churning out perfect pizza pies.

Top middle: Caesar salad with Sally's original dressing is a great opener while waiting for your pies to emerge from the oven.

Above middle: Sally's unusual and outrageously good white potato pie.

Top right: A sausage and pepperoni pizza, perfect for meat lovers.

Above right: Grown men have been known to weep for joy when they see this sign on Wooster Street in New Haven.

Then there's the garden special: fresh tomato, mozzarella, onion, zucchini, and basil. And finally, what may be Sally's most unusual (and wonderful) pizza, the white potato pie with thinly sliced potato wheels, onion, mozzarella, imported parmesan, and rosemary.

For starters, you may choose between a house or Caesar salad, both served with Sally's creamy dressing. Locally made Foxon Park sodas are the drink of choice here and are sold by the liter. Sally's Apizza on Wooster remains one of the most unique, best preserved, and most loved pizzerias in the country.

237 Wooster St., New Haven; 203-624-5271
sallysapizza.com

Sally's white potato pie was inspired by a pizza that Bobby Consiglio had on a trip to Rome.

Great southern cooking in a colorful, relaxed atmosphere

Lilly's is a great place to load up on fine Southern cooking from a restaurant and caterer that has been feeding the lucky residents of Windsor for more than 30 years. Housed in a handsome building with playful decorations out front and bright pastels within, this family-run, cafeteria-style, grab-n-go spot will not disappoint in terms of quantity and quality. And there's ice cream from the small stand under the same roof.

Lilly's came into being when Andre Lilly and his wife, Kimberly, decided to take the plunge into food service. They began as a catering operation, serving public and private functions in the greater Hartford area. They then expanded into the restaurant business with a walk-through line for customers to select their victuals from glassed-in steam tables loaded with huge portions of meat and vegetables. The restaurant is now Lilly's main business.

Foot traffic flows through Lilly's in one direction. Enter by the door on the left side of the building, where you'll initially encounter an antique organ with foot pedals and other vintage furniture. Photos of family and friends line the walls, giving a homey feel to the place. Advance further in line to reach what you've come for: a couple of long steam tables with attendants ready to dish up whatever you choose from the numerous offerings.

"Dinners," as they're called, are the way to go and are served throughout the day. They come in "meat-and-two" plastic containers with one large and two small sections for an entrée and two sides. Be

Be sure to leave room for a slice of Lilly's famous home-baked sweet potato pie.

Top left: Lilly's storefront is colorfully decorated with a variety of statuary and other kitsch.

Above left: Barbecued ribs, collard greens, black-eyed peas, and homemade corn bread.

Top right: A slice of sweet potato pie is always right for dessert.

Above right: Pinks and pastels dominate Lilly's inside dining area.

thankful there's a lid on these containers, as it's virtually impossible to finish all that Lilly's dishes up. Most people take their food to go, but there are a few brightly colored indoor booths, several tables with chairs, and a few café tables outside.

The most popular dinner is the fried chicken, followed closely by the barbecued ribs. Smothered pork chops and fried catfish are also big sellers. As for sides, take your pick of any two, including candied yams, collard greens, mac and cheese, black-eyed peas, potato salad, lima beans, and more. Portions are large, so don't order too much.

Everything washes down very nicely with a generous glassful of Michelle's sweet tea. And if you happen to be there in summertime, an ice cream cone from their adjacent parlor may be in order.

305 Windsor Ave., Windsor; 860-241-8132

World-class vegan in downtown Branford

This vegan standout celebrated its 10th anniversary in 2020, a testament to the restaurant's amazing meatless cuisine and to the power of great, inventive cooking that uses the healthiest of ingredients served in a beautiful Branford setting.

The name G-Zen reflects the core beliefs of co-owners Mark Shadle and Amy Beach Shadle: "G" stands for green business ethics and plant-based cuisine; "Zen" refers to "living mindfully, to be in a state of peace and balance in one's body." The Shadles live their dream and fulfill their mission through their dedicated work and practices at their Branford restaurant, their award-winning GMonkey vegan food truck, and their sustainable organic farm in nearby Durham.

The menu at G-Zen is broad and varied, filled with many intriguing vegan dishes, beverages, and desserts. Take your time, and study it carefully. There's lots to sample and enjoy here, and sharing with fellow diners is a great way to experience the broad range of offerings.

Start with the exotic drinks, many of them nonalcoholic. Fresh-pressed organic juices include such offerings as Zen Glow (organic celery, cucumber, apple, lemon, lime, beet, and ginger root) and Dr. Greens (organic celery, cucumber, kale, spinach, pear, lemon, ginger, and cilantro). Raw sake is the preferred alcohol base for G-Zen's sake-tini's, which include the Fire Island Zen-tini (organic coconut milk, coconut water, pineapple juice, and raw sake) and Purple Haze (organic Concord grape juice, joji berry juice, and cranberry with raw sake).

On to the victuals, it's imperative to try the G-Fries as one of the appetizers. G-Zen built its early reputation on these hand-cut sweet potato fries served with hickory smoked ketchup, initially doled out from their food truck. Another great starter is the Feisty Monkey: chilled whole-grain pasta with fresh herbs, a spicy peanut

Left: The Sublime vegan nachos are just that, and it makes a great opener for two people.

Left center: One of G-Zen's intoxicating exotic beverages, many of which are nonalcoholic.

Top right center: The Pure Radiance Salad features field greens and shredded vegetables over a scoop of raw, sprouted nut paté.

Above right center: The Downward Dog Bean Burrito with a side of G-Zen's hallmark sweet potato fries.

Right: G-Zen is housed in a beautifully restored building at a fork in Main Street facing downtown.

sauce, cilantro sauce, and cashew-based parmesan. The Zen Burger and the Downward Dog Bean Burrito are just two of the excellent sandwich selections.

The entrées are varied and substantial. Creole Tempeh—with caramelized onions, fire-roasted peppers, Creole sauce, mashed potatoes, local greens, and corn bread—is a local favorite. Then there's the Garden Guru, your choice of any 4 of 10 side dishes that include spanakopita, sauteed local greens, baked and seasoned tofu, and a black bean veggie patty.

If you've got room for dessert, the raw lemon lavender cheesecake is a good, refreshing choice as is the spiced carrot cake with a ginger frosting, chopped walnuts, and raisins. All desserts are, of course, dairy-free.

2 E. Main St., Branford; 203-208-0443
g-zen.com

The Shadles purchased a 270-year-old farm in nearby Durham. They're bringing it back to active farmland after 30 years of dormancy and growing much of G-Zen's produce there.

BRIDGEWATER CHOCOLATE

Handmade chocolates from humble beginnings blossom in Brookfield.

The Bridgewater Chocolate story is one of love, relocation, innovation, and, of course, chocolate. Theirs is a success story with a sweet and happy ending, and Connecticut is all the better for it.

Bridgewater founder Erik Landegren came to the United States from Sweden in 1987 to help open famed Manhattan restaurant Aquavit. In 1995, he moved with his wife to the western Connecticut town of Bridgewater to settle down and start raising a family. He took a job managing the quaint Bridgewater Village Store and began making chocolates using the Old World, handmade methods and ingredients he cherished from his childhood, along with such American ingredients as peanut butter.

His chocolates were an instant hit with the locals, and a mail-order business took off at the same time through serendipity and word of mouth. Not wanting to get bogged down in the business end of his chocolate-making enterprise, Landegren partnered with Andrew Blauner in 1999, and Bridgewater Chocolate came into being.

Today, Bridgewater has two retail outlets, one in their chocolate factory in neighboring Brookfield and the other in West Hartford. Both stores are a chocoholic's dream, with amazing displays and samples from Landegren's years of innovative chocolate-making.

Bridgewater offers a variety of chocolates, including turtles, toffees, caramels, truffles, peanut butter patties, and hazelnut pralines. Even

If you don't have the time to visit Bridgewater's retail outlets, be sure to check out their website, as anything they make can be ordered by mail and delivered to your door.

Left: Bridgewater Chocolate's West Hartford store.

Top middle: A very tempting five-pound box of handmade chocolates.

Above middle: A couple of Bridgewater's highly popular chocolate bars.

Right: A variety of Bridgewater chocolates and cocoas.

with the company's meteoric growth, all Bridgewater Chocolate products are still handmade. Their product lines include assorted chocolates, toffee assortments, tins (bite-sized chewy caramels and raisins), and cubes (bite-sized nuts and confections) in a variety of sizes and combinations.

Despite its industrial facade and its location in a business park, Bridgewater's main (factory) store is a feast for a chocolate-lover's eyes. Enter through the front door, and both sides of the lobby-like room are lined with seductive displays of handsomely boxed and wrapped chocolate treats. In back of the sales counter at the far end of the room is a window offering a view into the magical chocolate-making area, where confectioners and stainless-steel machines churn out the delectables on display out front. The West Hartford store is equally seductive, with exposed brick walls, built-in wooden display cases, and a glass-encased marble counter displaying the latest in Bridgewater's chocolate treats.

559 Federal Rd., Brookfield;
203-775-2286
(extension retail store: 227 Federal Rd.,
Brookfield; 203-648-9783)

12 LaSalle Rd., West Hartford;
860-570-0707
bridgewaterchocolate.com

LOBSTER LANDING

Hot buttered lobster rolls at their best

When you veer off Route 1 in downtown Clinton and drive toward the town's small, scenic marina, you eventually come face-to-face with a delightfully dilapidated little shack right on the water with its hand-painted sign above the door declaring in lopsided lettering that you're standing on the threshold of Lobster Landing.

Owners Enea and Cathie Bacci (Enea goes by his last name, "Bacci") have lovingly developed this little seaside shack into a culinary and cultural magnet for their adopted seaside hometown. They get their lobster from some 20 local lobster boats that offload at the harbor and on Lobster Landing's small dock, giving the place solid standing in the lobster roll world.

The menu is spare and direct and is posted on a simple, white wipe board in front of the small, open-air food counter just outside the shack: lobster rolls; sausage, pepper, and onion sandwiches; hot dogs; chips; soda; some ice cream; and little else. But the real (nay, the only) reason to come to Lobster Landing is for the meaty, buttery hot lobster roll for which it is best known.

The roll distinguishes itself in a couple of ways. First, it's chock-full of fresh-picked lobster meat (you can see them actually picking meat in the shack throughout the day); they certainly don't skimp, loading up the oversize bun until the lobster crowns out of the top.

The second thing is the bun itself. It's an Italian grinder roll, long and narrow, soft and fluffy; and it's toasted on a conventional, patio-type propane barbeque grill, adding a little bit of a crunchy sensation

Many consider Lobster Landing's hot buttered lobster roll to be the best in the state.

Left: The highly distinctive Lobster Landing shack on the Clinton waterfront.
Right: Two lobster rolls on toasted Italian sub rolls.

to the otherwise soft texture of the lobster meat. One lobster roll per person should be enough, but don't be surprised if you find yourself craving a second.

Bacci and Cathie have been in the restaurant business for many years, most recently owning an upscale Italian bistro in Southbury. Yearning for something simpler by the water, they stumbled upon Lobster Landing and purchased it in 1995. They haven't looked back and seemingly have no regrets about their foray into the lobster roll business.

Feel free to bring your own beer or wine to enjoy on Lobster Landing's harborside deck and picnic tables out front. Given the Italian flavor of the place, a nice pinot grigio or a bottle or two of Morelli beer might be in order for your sunny lobster roll feast by the sea.

152 Commerce St., Clinton; 860-669-2005

A deep-fried, dine-in-the-rough seafood shack on Noank harbor

Just down the road from Abbott's Lobster in the Rough is sister shack Costello's. This is the place in Noank for deep-fried seafood and great views of Noank harbor.

Costello's was opened in the mid-1990s by the Mears family, owners of Abbott's, to provide deep-fried options to hungry seafood seekers in Noank. Its location in the Noank boatyard adds greatly to the maritime feel of the place.

Costello's colorful blue-and-white awnings shade two levels of decks for dining. It's a dine-in-the-rough place, which means you order your food and pay for it through a window on the side of the shack, then pick it up on a plastic tray at a counter when your number is called.

Fried clams and clam strips are the name of the game here, along with other deep-fried goodies such as clam fritters, fish-and-chips, scallops, shrimp, oysters, and lobster tails. Costello's famed thin-cut French fries are a must-have accompaniment to any fried seafood order.

Sandwiches also abound here, like whole clam and clam strip rolls served on split-top buns, fish or shrimp tacos, a tasty fried-fish sandwich, and hot and cold lobster rolls. Should you wish to avoid the sea, try the juicy burger, the all-beef hot dogs, or chicken tacos.

Costello's is BYOB (always has been), so feel free to bring a cooler of your favorite alcoholic beverages and enjoy a sunny repast overlooking the picturesque harbor.

145 Pearl St., Noank; 860-572-2779
costellosclamshack.com

Top: A heaping plate of Costello's deep-fried clam strips.

Above left: The two levels of dining at Costello's mean plenty of room and great harbor views for visitors.

Above right: Costello's clam roll comes stuffed to the max with whole-belly clams.

BOHEMIAN PIZZA AND TACOS

1960s nostalgia along with giant fish tanks and great pizza

With wall-to-wall album covers blanketing the walls, canoes hanging from the ceilings, massive fish tanks, leopard-print booths, and a two-sided wood-burning fireplace in the middle of the main dining room, this labyrinthian eatery on Bantam Road seems to be the last thing you'd expect to find in bucolic rural Litchfield. Yet the wildly popular and completely unique Bohemian Pizza and Tacos pulls in crowds every day of the week year-round.

Co-owned by Jason MacKenzie and Gary Copeland since 2005, this beloved roadhouse brings in couples, families, bikers, teens, and seniors and mixes them all up in a dimly lit rec room atmosphere. MacKenzie runs the kitchen, and Copeland handles the business end of things; together they make a strong leadership team that's well known throughout the community.

In addition to the lively main dining room, there's an equally funky side room separated by a fish tank and a long, narrow, dimly lit bar festooned in kitsch, beckoning all to slake their thirst if they wish.

Pizza is the main draw on the menu, with more than 20 specialty pies to choose from. Try the Margarita, with fresh-sliced tomato, New Haven–style tomato sauce, fresh mozzarella, and fresh basil leaves sprinkled on top. The Buffalo Chicken is popular with meat eaters, with a spicy sauce base, shredded chicken, mozzarella, and

Huge fish tanks are embedded in the walls throughout Bohemian, mesmerizing diners with a variety of tropical fish.

Top left: Bohemian Pizza's funky facade hints at the fun within.

Above left: Bohemian's popular "Margarita" pizza.

Top middle: The Beet Salad comes with lots of goat cheese and a lemon-poppyseed dressing.

Above middle: Vinyl album covers and other memorabilia cover the walls throughout.

Right: Anything goes, decor-wise, with Bohemian's interior.

bleu cheese. And the white clam pizza draws raves for its olive oil base topped with mozzarella, finely chopped clams, fresh garlic, and crumbled bacon. All the pizza here comes in 18-inch pies and hews closely to the thin-crust, New Haven style made so popular along the Connecticut Shore. (Ten-inch, gluten-free, small sizes are also available upon request.)

Other notable menu choices include gourmet tacos and several fine salads, such as the caramelized pear salad, the tongue-in-cheek Shrute Farms beet salad, and the tart, tasty winter apple salad. There's a wide array of burgers, wraps, hard roll sandwiches, and even some pasta and Mexican dishes, but pizza is the way to go here.

Bohemian is a great place to have a drink or two, and there's plenty to choose from in the way of draft beers and ales, many of them from local brewers. On the mixed drink side, try the Apple Cider Sangria, dry white wine mixed with apple cider, ginger brandy, a dash of cinnamon whisky, and diced apples. Grab a seat at the bar or settle into a booth and soak in the bohemian vibes of this one-of-a-kind Litchfield treat.

342 Bantam Rd., Litchfield; 860-567-3980
bohemianpizza.com

FLANDERS FISH MARKET

A top-notch seafood market and a great restaurant to boot

What started in the early 1980s as a small mom-and-pop fish shop out of a house in East Lyme has blossomed into a famed restaurant, bar, demonstration kitchen, and retail seafood market. Founder Paul Formica, along with his late wife and their children, have built Flanders Fish Market into a coastal Connecticut institution, famed for its fresh fish, clear-broth clam chowder, beer-battered fish-and-chips, and much more. A request from a customer for fish-and-chips in the early days of the fish market prompted the Formicas to purchase a Fry-o-later, which launched a modest restaurant in back of the nascent seafood market.

Flanders is legendary for its beautifully stocked fresh seafood cases. They are front and center when you walk through the door, and has been much expanded from the original cottage. Slabs of fresh-cut finned fish and buckets of fresh shellfish are on display, along with a case of tantalizing prepared seafood specialties, such as stuffed shrimp, crab cakes, mussel salad, smoked bluefish, herring in wine, seafood salad, and lobster pot pies.

The friendly, knowledgeable staff behind the counter dotes on your every seafood need. In addition to carrying large supplies of the usual New England cornucopia of fish and shellfish, Flanders also specializes in seasonal and special-order fish, such as blackfish, blue marlin, arctic char, mahi mahi, shark, smelts, red snapper, shad and shad roe (a local favorite), grouper, and striped bass.

In the back of the dining room, Flanders has a unique "Demo Dining" setup, with a demonstration kitchen at one end of the restaurant's dining room. It's equipped with television cameras and screens around the dining room, so patrons can watch the chefs at work on Friday and Saturday evenings.

Top left: The Flanders seafood case is always packed with fresh fish.

Above left: The beer-battered fish-and-chips that Flanders is famous for.

Top right: A beautifully presented hot buttered lobster roll, a Flanders specialty.

Above right: Fresh shellfish on display in iced buckets is a sight to behold.

Flanders also offers a unique "Chef's Table" experience, where groups are prepared a gourmet five-course seafood meal in the demonstration kitchen. Olivia Formica, one of Paul's daughters, is head chef at Flanders and a graduate of the Culinary Institute of America. She is often the one cooking for the Captain's Table, along with her father, and the dishes are splendid. Olivia will explain everything she's doing while you enjoy each course and a glass of wine. It's a great way to enjoy a meal with family or a group of friends or coworkers.

22 Chesterfield Rd., East Lyme; 860-739-8866
flandersfish.com

Cappy's Chowder was one of the market's initial successes. The Formicas adapted it from a local fisherman's recipe.

Dottie's for donuts, meat loaf, pot pie, and more

In Woodbury, "D" stands for Dottie's, and it also stands for donuts—one of the trademark offerings at Dottie's Diner. Done up in a snappy 1950s motif, Dottie's goes well beyond its time-capsule appearance to serve up some of the best traditional and contemporary diner food in the state.

Located on a rise above South Main Street, Dottie's draws fans from all over western Connecticut. Roadfood (a book and website that helps you find the best in regional food across the United States) founders Jane and Michael Stern are longtime fans of the place and once declared that Dottie's donuts are the nation's best.

Owner Dorie Sperry has poured a ton of love into her diner, having bought it in 2006 from the Phillips family, who had owned it since the 1930s. Locals held their collective breath, waiting to see what the new owner would do. Sperry wisely kept serving the diner's most famous fare, including its doughnuts and its equally famed chicken pot pie.

Over time, Dorie, who previously held management positions at the famed Mayflower Inn in Washington Depot, has put her own stamp on the place. She has introduced a number of new dishes, such as a smoked salmon breakfast platter, a version of the chicken pot pie that includes lots of healthy vegetables, a vegetable risotto, and pan-seared salmon with wild rice and grilled asparagus.

Back to the donuts. The Phillips clan started the tradition of making fresh donuts daily, and Sperry has upheld the tradition. Every day, you'll find such flavors as cinnamon sugar, chocolate- or vanilla-dipped, powdered, jelly, and Boston cream donuts. The texture is dense, the flavor is rich, and the toppings are unforgettable. Many

Top left: Dottie's serpentine counter invites everyone for breakfast, lunch, or dinner.

Above left: A plate of Dottie's world-famous donuts, made fresh in the kitchen every day.

Middle: Dottie's grand entryway overlooking South Main Street in Woodbury.

Top right: Dottie's chicken pot pie, a longtime customer favorite.

Above right: Meatloaf, mashed potatoes, and fresh vegetables, all smothered in homemade gravy. Heaven on earth.

customers stop by and grab a bag of donuts at the cash register and then take off for what will certainly be a happier day.

No diner is complete without pie, and Dottie's offers fresh-baked pies by the slice and whole daily. There are about a half dozen fruit pies and cream pies on any given day. Just remember to preorder a day or two in advance if you want a whole one to take home. Day-old cinnamon donuts are reconstituted into a wonderful bread pudding that would make any Brit proud.

Grab a stool at the serpentine counter or settle into a booth for breakfast, lunch, or dinner at this top-rated, expertly managed eatery on the edge of the Antiques Capital of Connecticut. The coffee's always hot and fresh-brewed, and the cheerful, professional waitstaff will make you feel right at home.

787 Main St. S., Woodbury; 203-263-2516
dottiesdiner.com

LONG WHARF FOOD TRUCKS

A little bit of Latin America on the New Haven waterfront

When motoring on I-95 through New Haven, you can't miss the caravan of colorful food trucks lined up on Long Wharf Drive between the interstate and Long Island Sound. They're out there year-round, serving up great meals and snacks of all sorts—especially those of a Latin American nature.

The food trucks at Long Wharf are part of a group of New Haven food vendors operating under the name Food Truck Paradise. They have other setups around the city, but Long Wharf has the largest concentration and the biggest following among food truck fans.

On any given day, especially in the warmer months, there may be a dozen or more food trucks lined up bumper to bumper vying for your business. Stroll by and peruse the colorful menus on the sides of the trucks, then circle back and order from the truck(s) of your choosing. The atmosphere is that of an open-air market, with lots of interactions between vendors and diners. Here's just a sampling of the trucks that make regular appearances at Long Wharf:

Ixtapa Tacos #1: Specializes in Mexican tacos and burritos, tostadas, and quesadillas, each loaded with your choice of pork, sausage, chicken, tongue, or barbecue. Wash it all down with a Mexican Coke or other soft drink.

Now We're Smokin': This Long Wharf mainstay serves up Southern-style barbecue from its adorable red log cabin on wheels. Their smoker sits under a roof on one end of the trailer and churns out copious quantities of ribs, pulled pork, beef brisket, and barbecued chicken. Other goodies include grilled hot dogs, baked mac and cheese, and smoky baked beans.

Tripletas & More: This primarily Puerto Rican food truck painted red, white, and blue and flying the Puerto Rican flag serves

Left: Sugary churros are served piping hot and enjoyed by the bagful.

Top middle: Ixtapa is one of the more popular Mexican food trucks on Long Wharf.

Above middle: Soft tacos and burritos go well with a Mexican Coke, sweetened with sugar cane.

Top right: Mexican street corn is typically offered by several trucks on any given day.

Above right: Sweeney's Hot Dog King, the first truck to call Long Wharf home, is a permanent fixture nearly every day.

up *pinchos* (meat on a stick), mofongo, churrasco with tostones, empanadas, nonalcoholic piña coladas, and *carne frita* (fried pork chunks). Large cups filled with chopped fruit are also popular.

Sweeney's Hot Dog King: For those shying away from Latin American and other ethnic foods, there's this hot dog truck, the first one on Long Wharf, that does regular pups off the grill for a couple of bucks, and a dressed-up Georgia Dog for a dollar more. Cold cans of soda and hot coffee round out the menu offerings.

Sandwich El Cubano: In addition to all the standard Latino treats, this truck prides itself on its Sandwich Cubano—pork, ham, cheese, pickles, and mustard between thin-sliced, lightly toasted Cuban bread.

351 Long Wharf Dr., New Haven;
streetfoodnhv.com

Parent company Street Food New Haven also has food truck spots by Yale-New Haven Hospital, the New Haven Green, and Sachem Street by Yale University.

B. F. CLYDE'S CIDER MILL (page 26)

ESSEX SHAD BAKE (page 184)

GLENWOOD DRIVE-IN (page 178)

BOHEMIAN PIZZA AND TACOS (page 76)

MILLWRIGHT'S (page 154)

GRANO ARSO (page 38)

BUFALINA (page 104)

COSTELLO'S (page 74)

JESSICA'S GARDEN (page 134)

LAUREL DINER (page 136)

ANTOJOS (page 10)

THE PANTRY (page 180)

WILLIMANTIC BREWING COMPANY (page 60)

FLANDERS FISH MARKET (page 78)

UNION LEAGUE CAFE (page 56)

Cheeses from around the world and so much more

Anchoring one end of a colorful strip mall in Old Saybrook, Fromage Fine Foods and Coffees is almost certainly the best cheese shop in the state. With more than 250 types of cheeses from nearly 20 countries, no other cheesemonger can come close in terms of variety and quality. This place is a cheese lover's dream come true.

Fromage opened its doors in 1992 when Old Saybrook native Christine Chesanek launched the business in a small shared space with Atlantic Seafood about a mile down the road. She modeled the shop on those found in Europe, where gourmet cheeses may be sampled and procured in a friendly, professional atmosphere with knowledgeable staff. After some 15 to 20 years in its original location, Chesanek made the move to larger quarters and hasn't looked back.

In its current expanded quarters, Fromage has become a purveyor of all sorts of gourmet food items. In addition to its amazing cheese selections, there are cases of charcuterie, cured olives, foie gras, and other delicacies. Scattered throughout the rest of the store is a labyrinth of shelves displaying pastas, olive oils, jams, teas, cookies, crackers, and more. Gourmet whole bean and ground coffees round out the amazing offerings.

The cheese takes center stage, however. Behind the counter is a massive blackboard displaying the names of all the cheeses currently available, organized by country. Making selections can be overwhelming, but Christine's aproned, knowledgeable staff are extremely helpful and can offer up cheese samples to help you decide.

Top: The blackboard behind the counter lists the more than 200 cheeses available at Fromage.

Above left: There's lots to enjoy at this fine-foods specialty shop—especially the amazing selections of cheese.

Above right: Many of the fine cheeses are on display at the front counter.

In addition to dozens of world-renowned cheeses from France, Italy, Spain, England, Holland, California, Vermont, and other cheese-making meccas, there's an amazing variety of local cheeses, such as those from the famed Arethusa Dairy in Litchfield and wonderfully fresh homemade mozzarella and ricotta from Liuzzi Gourmet Foods in North Haven.

873 Boston Post Rd., Old Saybrook; 860-388-5750
fromagefinefoods.com

Hand-crafted pizza in a cozy cottage setting

Blink and you'll miss this gem of a pizza place on the Boston Post Road in Guilford—and you certainly don't want to miss it.

Bufalina is the creation of husband-and-wife team Melissa Pellegrino and Matt Scialabba. The couple spent four years traveling around Italy, cooking at agriturismos and learning the fine craft of baking in wood-fired brick ovens. Upon returning to the States, they opened their pizzeria in a small, red colonial cottage not much larger than a couple of toolsheds combined.

There's a 10-seat, L-shaped marble counter that wraps around the cramped kitchen/brick oven area and one small table that can accommodate two hungry diners off to the side. Everyone has a ringside seat to witness the wonder of pizza-making at its most elemental, as Melissa and Matt work their magic behind the counter while carrying on banter with their clientele.

The menu is as simple and alluring as the surroundings. Start with the salad special, which changes weekly and typically consists of mixed greens, a variety of farm-fresh vegetables, toasted seeds, shaved Italian hard cheeses, and homemade balsamic vinaigrette dressings. One salad is plenty for two people.

Pizza is the main show here. The namesake Bufalina pizza, featuring Buffalo mozzarella, San Marzano tomatoes, and strips of fresh basil, is a must-have. The crust on all Bufalina's pizzas is soft and chewy with a bit of burnt bits around the edges.

Other pizzas on the regular menu include the Margherita (mozzarella and scamorza cheeses, San Marzano tomatoes, and basil), Spinaci (wilted spinach, mozzarella, Gorgonzola dolce, and fontina cheeses), Broccoli (charred broccoli, buffalo mozzarella, garlic-herb oil, and grated pecorino), Patate (herb-roasted potatoes,

Top left: Salads are made fresh and change weekly.

Above left: A pizza baking in the rustic oven, the heart and soul of Bufalina.

Top middle: Bufalina's owners, Matt Scialabba and Melissa Pellegrino, and their wood-fired brick oven.

Above middle: A sausage pie, baked to perfection.

Right: Bufalina's tiny, modest home on the Boston Post Road in Guilford.

fontina cheese, and spicy Calabrian sausage), and Tre Carni (tomatoes, mozzarella, lightly smoked prosciutto, *salame piccante* [spicy cured salami], and sausage) for meat lovers. Each day features special pizzas, such as a roasted red pepper pizza with sausage and arugula and a pork ragu pizza with chestnuts and prunes.

The highlight of the dessert menu is a petite Nutella Pizza with the namesake hazelnut spread and powdered sugar.

Melissa and Matt have created a charming eatery that engenders conversations between patrons as well as an amazing menu that exudes the warmth and love that the couple has for their hearth-baked cuisine.

1070 Boston Post Rd., Guilford; (203) 458-1377
bufalinact.com

The 900-degree, wood-fired brick oven turns out personal-sized, irregular-shaped, thin-crust pizzas in less than two minutes, such is the intensity of the oven's heat.

CITY FISH MARKET

If it swims in the sea, City Fish most likely has it.

This Greek American, family-owned seafood market and restaurant dominates the seafood world in central Connecticut as well as much of the rest of the state. The market's distinctive yellow trucks, with their golden fishhook logo on the sides, can be seen throughout southern New England, making deliveries to restaurants and quality food retailers year-round.

City Fish began life on Main Street in Hartford in the 1930s. It later moved to Front Street, and then finally to its current home south of the city in Wethersfield. Five generations of the Anagnos family have built City Fish into the juggernaut it is today.

City Fish also has its own excellent retail seafood market. The retail floor sits in the midst of a large, warehouse-like space where fish deliveries and orders are processed and transported for wholesale customers on dollies, which are wheeled across concrete floors that are regularly sprayed down with lots of water to keep things fresh, cool, and clean.

And what a retail market it is. The massive, glass-encased seafood counter is stuffed chockablock daily with all sorts of wonderfully fresh seafood from City Fish's 70,000-cubic-foot cold-storage room. (There's also a 100,000-cubic-foot deep freezer used mostly for the wholesale business.) You probably won't find cheaper, better swordfish steaks in the area, with specials on the hand-cut fillets featured regularly.

Around the corner from the seafood counter and next to the lobster tanks is a seafood stand featuring fine fish-and-chips baskets

> There's a 5,000-gallon lobster pound that regularly stocks "bugs" weighing anywhere from one to 10 pounds.

Top left: City Fish's 30-plus-foot-long seafood case offers a vast array of fresh seafood goodies.

Above left: Cold and hot lobster rolls are both available at City Fish for indoor or to-go dining.

Middle: Fresh shellfish from New England and Canadian waters are always available.

Top right: Be sure to grab some deep-fried seafood for lunch or dinner while at City Fish.

Above right: It's easy to spot City Fish Market's distinctive blue and yellow building on the Silas Deane Highway.

and regionally famous lobster rolls served both warm with butter or chilled with mayo. Through a door and just behind the back wall of the retail seafood counter, you will find an air-conditioned dining room with tables, televisions, beer, and wine. It can accommodate up to 100 people and doubles as a banquet facility for special occasions.

City Fish's high volume allows it to get top-quality fish and shellfish from its suppliers. The company runs its own semitruck to and from the main seafood market in Boston three times a week. In addition, numerous other regional, national, and even international suppliers do a lot of business with City Fish. This benefits the retail market through plentiful supplies and extended seasons for often hard-to-get items.

Stop by City Fish Market's bright-blue building with yellow awnings on the Silas Deane Highway, where you can stock up on plenty of fresh seafood and prepared foods of all sorts—and stick around for lunch or an early dinner.

884 Silas Deane Hwy., Wethersfield; 860-522-3129
cfishct.com

What classic drive-ins are all about

If you long for the the halcyon days of 1950s hot rods, slicked-back hair, poodle skirts, and car-side service, pay a visit to the Sycamore Drive-In in Bethel to experience a neon-soaked roadside stand that serves up heaping helpings of great drive-in food and nostalgia.

The Sycamore isn't one of those faux drive-in restaurants concocted by a marketing group to cash in on 1950s nostalgia. It's the real deal, with roots going back to 1948 when it was founded by Joe Keller, who named the restaurant after a tall sycamore tree next to the building.

There are two dining rooms at the Sycamore. The front room contains the open kitchen, which sits on the other side of a long counter that's lined with chrome and vinyl stools that date back to the drive-in's founding. There are also several wooden booths and tables and lots of vintage photos on the walls. The back dining room features Formica-top tables, a black-and-white checkerboard vinyl floor, and all sorts of fun memorabilia from the mid-1900s, such as antique gasoline pumps and model cars.

On the menu, you'll find many of the standard items you'd expect to find at any classic drive-in. Hamburgers at the Sycamore are called Steakburgers, as they're made from round steak freshly ground on the premises every day and served on toasted, buttered buns. There are a dozen variations on the burgers, so there's plenty to choose from. The Sycamore's crowning burger achievement is the Dagwood—a perfectly grilled ground steak patty with American cheese and every condiment you can think of.

Grilled franks are another popular item, especially the Sycamore Frank with mustard, relish, raw onion, sauerkraut, and bacon. There's a nice selection of deep-fried seafood and salad plates that come loaded with sliced beets, tomatoes, cucumbers, cole slaw, and more.

Top left: The two dining areas are done up with all sorts of 1950s memorabilia, including a life-sized likeness of the famed rebel without a cause, James Dean.

Above left: Car hop service is still available at the Sycamore. Just flash your headlights when you pull in, and someone will be out (not on roller skates, though) to take your order.

Top right: The Steakburger Plate features onion rings, bacon, and cheese between bun and patty.

Above right: The Sycamore Drive-In, looking much as it did when it first opened in 1948.

In keeping with one of the best drive-in traditions, the Sycamore still has curb service. Just flash your headlights, and a server will be out to take your order. Every Saturday night from May through September is Cruise Night, when vintage cars fill the parking lot and gearheads gather to admire each other's rides. Live music is often part of the mix.

282 Greenwood Ave., Bethel; 203-748-2716
sycamoredrivein.com

The Sycamore brews its own root beer. It always has and probably always will. Stop in for a black cow or other ice cream treat, and step back in time at Bethel's best known dining spot.

It's all about "The Bomb."

Ford Lobster's signature Lobster Bomb put this modest dockside restaurant/shack on the culinary map several years ago, and thousands of curious customers have beaten a path to Ford's ever since. The Bomb—a hollowed-out bread *boule* filled with chunks of lobster meat and topped with thick, creamy lobster bisque—typically runs north of $40, but it's a seafood feast for two or more hungry customers. It's the main reason to seek out this hard-to-find place.

Summer is the best time to come to Ford's, as their large patio area by the dock is populated with umbrellaed tables overlooking the small harbor filled with pleasure craft. Boaters love this place and can pull up to the dock, place an order, and get onboard service.

Ford's began life as a gas dock and bait shop for boaters and anglers, and then began selling live lobsters to the locals. About 10 years ago, they added a lobster roll cart to the mix, and things took off from there. An indoor, year-round restaurant was established, and seasonal tables were put out by the dock. The menu is very lobster-centric, with such dishes as lobster risotto, lobster thermidor, boiled whole lobster, lobster mac and cheese, and lobster Alfredo. The Bomb and hot buttered lobster rolls, however, remain the most popular items.

In addition to all the lobster offerings, salmon, scallops, ahi tuna, and cod are other popular dishes. Lunchtime features a variety of

Ford's is extremely popular and crowded during the summer months, and there are no reservations. So, bring plenty of patience and a good attitude, and hope for fair weather!

Top left: One of several shacks on Ford's dock.

Above left: The Lobster Bomb, a killer combination of lobster meat and bisque, packed and poured into a warm boule.

Top right: Ford's hot buttered lobster roll rivals the Lobster Bomb in popularity.

Above right: Alfresco dining in season is the way to go at Ford's.

sandwiches, including a lobster BLT, lobster and avocado grilled cheese, blackened fish tacos, a crab cake sandwich, a Reuben, a burger, and a chicken club sandwich.

Back to the Bomb: You get a half pound of fresh-picked lobster meat, either warm and buttered or chilled with mayo and celery, stuffed into a boule. For a few dollars more (and it's worth it), they'll ladle a generous amount of lobster bisque into the cavity. It's messy but fun, and the seaside setting seals the deal, making it one of the premier treats to be had on the Connecticut Shore.

15 Riverview Ave., Noank; 860-536-2842
fordslobster.com

LOG HOUSE RESTAURANT

A woodsy getaway for the entire family

Located on a quiet stretch of Route 44 between New Hartford and Winsted, the Log House Restaurant has the look and feel of an old-fashioned roadhouse supper club, which is always a welcome sight when seeking out a warm and friendly place to grab a meal.

Founded by Mary Dileo in the early 1970s, the Log House was initially a modest eatery in a smallish cedar log building. In the intervening years, the restaurant has expanded to nearly 5,000 square feet with three different dining areas. The Dileo family still owns it.

The Log House boasts family-style dining in a homey atmosphere. Pine-paneled walls and cozy booths and tables abound in the two dining rooms and counter area, offering a variety of seating choices. Quaint wagon wheel chandeliers hang in the main dining room, and there's plenty of memorabilia on the walls throughout the restaurant.

Breakfast is the most popular meal, and it's served throughout the day. Standout items include the ham steak and three eggs with home fries and toast, the New York steak and three eggs with the same sides, and the belt-busting 2×2×2×2: two eggs, two pancakes or French toast, two strips of bacon, and two breakfast sausages.

Burgers and sandwiches rule throughout the lunch and dinner hours, with the Reubens (corned beef or pastrami) particularly tasty and affordable. The Outlaw Burger, with cheddar cheese, bacon, and homemade chili on top, is the burger of choice. Full dinners with potato and fresh vegetables include the traditional Yankee pot roast and the crispy fried chicken.

110 New Hartford Rd., Barkhamsted; 860-379-8937
theloghouserestaurant.com

112

Top: The Log House's distinctive exterior lives up to its name.

Above: The beef patty melt on grilled rye is one of many fine sandwich selections at the Log House.

Meaty lobster rolls at scenic Saybrook Point

This seasonal snack shack, an offshoot of Old Saybrook's renowned Liv's Oyster Bar, resides next to Harbor One marina at Saybrook Point. The cottage-like, shingled shack has no indoor seating, a limited menu, and one of the best lobster rolls in the state.

Liv's Shack originated from weekend stands at farmer's markets and the popular autumn Durham Fair. Liv's chef/owner John Brescio opened the brick-and-mortar shack in 2014 at the request of the marina's owners, who had a shack but no eatery.

"No Mayo!" is the battle cry here, as Liv's Shack specializes in hot buttered lobster rolls and not the chilled type with mayo. The workers even have the slogan emblazoned on their T-shirts. (Truth told, Liv's says they'll do a cold roll for you if you ask.)

The much-touted hot roll is excellent, consisting of a fresh-baked brioche bun with loads of butter-sauteed lobster meat packed within. Simplicity seems to be the watchword here, and Liv's lobster roll succeeds magnificently. Be sure to pair your roll with a side of Liv's famous truffle fries, cooked in super-clean oil and suffused with tasty truffle oil and a light sprinkling of granulated cheese.

Picnic tables surround two sides of the shack, most with umbrellas, making for a nice spot to enjoy your repast. Other menu items to consider are burgers and hot dogs cooked up on the griddle, lobster grilled cheese, and a Cajun mahi Brescia taco.

Liv's Shack is a great place to bring the kids, with its outdoor setting and its proximity to the highly popular miniature golf course at the nearby town park and historic site at the point. The wee ones can run around in fenced-in security while waiting for their meals to

Top: A warm buttered lobster roll and truffle fries ready for devouring.

Above left: Liv's Shack, serving up lobster rolls and more by the Old Saybrook waterfront.

Above right: Two warm buttered lobster rolls on brioche buns and truffle fries on the side.

arrive. Griddled hot dogs, hamburgers, cheeseburgers, grilled cheese, and chicken tenders all come in age-appropriate portions, and there's a fine selection of Foxon Park sodas in the cooler inside the shack. All the kids' meals come with a side of french fries. Liv's is BYO for adults who wish to imbibe.

26 Bridge St., Old Saybrook; 860-391-8353
livsshack.com

SEL

Giving pizza in New Haven a run for the money

Not all great pizza in Connecticut comes from New Haven. Case in point is Roseland Apizza of Derby, which is well into its fifth generation of loving family ownership in the Naugatuck River valley.

The Lucarelli family opened Roseland in 1935 in a plain, white, frame house where it remains today, looking pretty much like it did 85 years ago. Cofounder Lina Lucarelli became the de facto neighborhood mama to her extended family and to the many patrons who frequented (and still frequent) this Italian American staple. She watched over her beloved restaurant for decades and also started Roseland's tradition of putting a rotund boule of home-baked bread out for every table of customers.

The tradition continues to this day, but beware: as tempting as it is to indulge in this fine opener, resist the urge and save room for the massive quantities of great cooking to come from Roseland's kitchen.

The house salad is big, loaded with roasted red bell pepper, pepperoni, olives, provolone cheese, and lots of lettuce. The small family-style salad is enough of an opener for four, and the large version will easily satisfy at least six hungry diners. Also great for starters are the clams casino and the garlic bread, which comes loaded with roasted peppers, prosciutto, and mozzarella cheese.

The open-space dining room has about a dozen booths. The walls are lined with wonderfully nostalgic photos, and there's a blackboard suspended on the back wall that lists the numerous specialty pizzas (many of the white variety, loaded with seafood) as

When ordering your starters and dinners, you'll be asked if you'd like everything to be bathed in garlic, and there's only one correct response: *yes!*

116

Top left: The white fresh-shucked clam pizza is a must-have, especially for first-time visitors.

Above left: The family-style salads are loaded with lots of Italian goodies and are large enough for four to six people.

Above middle: Be sure to check out the specialty pizzas board on the back wall, as it changes almost daily and features some of the best pies.

Top right: Roseland's neon sign over the front door has been lighting up the night for decades.

Above right: The Roseland Special pizza features loads of Italian sausage and mushrooms.

well as the dinner specials. Entrées are enormous, and you're almost expected to take home much of what's served.

Roseland's best-known pizza is probably its white fresh-shucked clam pizza. One look at the clams tells you they aren't lying—fresh out of the shells, garlicky, and succulent. For those who prefer a red pie, try the Roseland Special, loaded with sausage and mushrooms and lots of mozzarella. The white shrimp pie types are numerous. Study the blackboard and take your pick; you can't really go wrong.

Entrées are of the straightforward Italian American variety— ravioli; spaghetti; baked ziti; chicken, veal, or eggplant parmigiana; and lasagna. Quantities are massive; take-home is almost mandatory.

350 Hawthorne Ave., Derby; 203-735-0494

Three hot dog sizes to match anyone's appetite

With its red and yellow carnival colors, fluorescent lighting, 1950s decor, and prime location on the busy Berlin Turnpike, Doogie's is a classic American hot dog stand in every sense. Offering more than a dozen hot dog variations (including the famous two-footer), 10 burger styles, fried seafood, and sides galore, there's plenty to enjoy here in the way of classic American food.

Doogie's roots stretch back to the early 1980s when it began life as a barbecue and seafood place called the Char-Bar in Ogunquit, Maine. Upon moving to Connecticut, the barbecue was dropped, the seafood stuck around, and the owners ramped up their offerings of hot dogs and hamburgers. In the intervening years, Doogie's has blossomed as a place where you can get a dog or a burger pretty much any way you want it, and the seafood remains a source of pride.

Upon entering the low-slung, single-story building, the first thing you're likely to notice is the string of 45-rpm vinyl records wrapped along the wainscoting in the dining area. Most of the vintage discs are 1950s and 1960s hits such as "Chantilly Lace," "Yesterday," and "Tequila." Posters of Elvis and vintage mid-century cars complete the classic-rock theme.

Doogie's is an old-fashioned, order-at-the-counter place. The wall-mounted menu with its many choices can be intimidating, so feel free to step aside and take some time to study it before ordering. (This place likes to get cute with the language, so fries are "fryze," cheese is "cheeze," mushrooms are "'shrooms," and so on.)

First up are the hot dogs. There are three different sizes: 10 inches, 16 inches, and 24 inches (the two-footer). You can get your dog plain or with the basic toppers of sauerkraut, chili, or cheeze.

From there, the specialty dogs and combinations are seemingly endless—Kelly, College, Dixie, Turnpike, Boston, Reuben, and

Top left: 45-rpm vinyl discs of numerous classic rock and soul songs line the dining room walls.

Above left: Doogie's colorful dining room and expansive order counter.

Middle: Doogie's famous two-footer hot dog dressed with the works.

Top right: The Doogie's sign is hard to miss on the busy Berlin Turnpike.

Above right: Doogie's famed Rodeo Burger seemingly delivers all the food groups.

Tijuana. All the wieners are long and thin, hanging out of both ends of their split-top buns, and grilled to a light crisp.

Burgers are fewer in number but equally colorful: the Boomer, Bacon Bleu, Swiss 'Shroom, Rodeo, Caveman, and more. Pair any of these sandwich delights with fryze, slaw, 'shrooms, baked beans, or fried dough.

Don't forget the seafood. Doogie's does a surprisingly good job for an inland operation with excellent fried clams and strips, fish-and-chips, and various fried seafood platters.

2525 Berlin Trpk., Newington; 860-666-3647
doogieshotdogs.com

Doogie's serves locally famous Grote & Weigel hot dogs,
made by a Connecticut company dating back to the 1890s.

Marvelous breakfasts and exotic game are menu highlights.

There aren't many places in Connecticut that regularly serve alligator, but the deceptively named Corner Restaurant of Milford is one of them. The name's deceptive because (1) the restaurant isn't actually on a corner; and (2) corner restaurants tend to be plain, simple coffee-shop-type eateries, yet Milford's Corner Restaurant is anything but plain and simple.

Founded in 1997 by Michelle and Amer Lebel, this is the little breakfast place that could. After struggling in its first few years, the Corner hit its stride with a highly innovative menu. Some say their stuffed French toast—French bread split and filled with fresh fruit, then battered and fried, then bathed in orange zest, nutmeg, cinnamon, and real maple syrup—elevated the Corner to all-star status. It remains the most popular dish on the menu.

And there's so much more. Take the "Duck," for example. Probably the second most famous item on the menu, this breakfast sandwich features South Indian spiced pulled duck wrapped in a bacon-layered flour tortilla that's also stuffed with scrambled eggs and melted cheese.

Not exotic enough for you? Say hello to perhaps the third most popular treat—South African Hash, a spicy beef and lentil hash over poached eggs and an English muffin *then* topped with Bernaise sauce and crispy shaved potato strings. There are Cuban pork breakfast tacos, blackened eggs, and several different types of omelets, including a portobello, spinach, and feta omelet for those seeking something vegetarian.

If your culinary compass is pointing toward stuffed French toast, the best-known and most popular version is the Peaches and Cream, stuffed and topped with the two namesake ingredients. A close second is the Apple, Cinnamon, Raisin, and Cream Cheese Stuffed

Left: Stuffed French toast is the most popular dish at the Corner. Here is the Apple, Cinnamon, Raisin, and Cream Cheese version.

Middle: Antique furniture and nostalgic kitsch fill the Corner Restaurant's warm interior.

Top right: The Corner Restaurant in downtown Milford.

Above right: The Corner's famed Duck sandwich, filled with South Indian spiced duck, cheese, and eggs wrapped in bacon and a crispy tortilla.

French Toast, a trio of thick-cut French bread slices stuffed and bathed with all the aforementioned goodies.

Fear not if you are feeling less adventurous, as there are plenty of more pedestrian offerings to choose from. Buttermilk pancakes, a nice ham and cheese omelet with home fries, and a fresh fruit plate with vanilla yogurt are appealing, and there are several vegan dishes. The lunch sandwich offerings are uniformly solid, but breakfast is the way to go here.

As for the alligator, it makes regular appearances in the Corner's jambalaya. There are also more out-there game offerings, such as zebra, wild boar, and other things not normally found anywhere; get on the Corner's email list to receive notifications when such exotica comes up as specials.

105 River St., Milford; 203-882-1150
thecornerbrunch.com

Want to find out what's going on in Milford? Grab a seat, order a cup of coffee or a meal, settle in, and listen to the chatter.

DONAHUE'S CLAM CASTLE

The perfect respite after a day at Hammonasset State Beach

Strategically located on US Route 1 next to Hammonasset Beach State Park, Donahue's Clam Castle has for decades been a must-stop before, during, or after a day at the beach. Housed in a squat, one-story building lined with windows on two sides, this venerable deep-fried seafood spot is beloved by locals and tourists alike.

Founded in the early 1960s as "The Clam Castle" by an owner known to customers only as "Art," the shack has remained true to its original mission of serving up great fried seafood to hungry beachgoers and locals. Current owners Dave and Sloane Donahue brought some much-needed upgrades to the eatery when they took over several years ago, yet it still looks pretty much the same as it has for more than half a century. Denizens of the Connecticut Shore love their seaside traditions, and the Castle's sentimental value has not been lost on the Donahues.

Queue up at the order counter inside, which features a large wall-mounted menu for easy perusal. Take your time and order carefully—there's plenty of good stuff to choose from. Fried clams are a must-have, either the whole-belly variety or the strips. Each comes in platter form (with fries, coleslaw, tartar sauce, and lemon); as a roll in a toasted, top-split bun; or as a large side order. The whole bellies are melt-in-your-mouth good, with light breading and full-on clam flavor. The strips are fried to a golden-brown crispness and overflow the basket they're served in.

> Madison resident Jacques Pepin is a fan of the Clam Castle and has been known to dine here from time to time.

Left: The lobster bisque is thick, creamy, and loaded with lobster meat.

Top middle: The Clam Castle likes to show off its beautiful landscaping in the summertime.

Above middle: Fried clam strips are piled atop a bed of fries in the clam strip platter.

Right: The hot buttered lobster roll is a favorite of several food critics.

The Donahues are equally proud of their fish-and-chips platters, which feature fresh fillets dipped and coated in panko or broiled or blackened—unconventional yet tasty ways to enjoy this traditional seafood treat. Fish tacos are also on the menu, featuring seasoned cod, pico de gallo, fresh cilantro, cabbage slaw, and lime crema.

The hot buttered lobster roll here is a favorite of many local customers, with its five ounces of fresh-picked meat warmed in melted butter and then stuffed in a toasted bun. Chowders come in creamy New England or clear-broth Rhode Island styles. The lobster bisque is a house specialty, rich and creamy and loaded with fresh lobster flavor.

There are about 10 booths for indoor seating, a couple of tables in front by the road, and several sheltered picnic tables in the back. Feel free to bring your own libations, as the Castle is BYOB.

1324 Boston Post Rd., Madison; 203-245-4911
clamcastlect.com

A great, big helping of Poland's finest

Staropolska is the beating heart of New Britain's Little Poland neighborhood. The restaurant serves as a focal point for the local Polish community, offering a gathering place for Poles to enjoy a beer or two and some fine Polish cuisine.

Housed in a solid, mid–20th century brick building, Staropolska offers a modest, comfortable dining room with about 15 tables and booths and a bar area where locals congregate to sip beer and vodka and enjoy international soccer matches on TV. The atmosphere is relaxed, warm, and friendly, and the waitstaff makes you feel right at home.

Start your Staropolska experience with a Polish beer or a shot of Polish vodka. There are several types of each. A bottle of Heveliusz beer is a good place to start for the uninitiated. A chilled shot of Zubrowka vodka also whets the appetite for the massive portions of fine Polish food to come.

All the food coming from the kitchen derives from family recipes lovingly curated by Bogdan and Margaret Malinowski, the longtime owners. A good place to start your Malinowski-inspired Polish feast is with a cup or bowl of one of the homemade soups. The red borscht is a crimson broth with meat dumplings bobbing on the surface. Beef tripe soup and pickle soup are other enticing options.

Pickled herring is a popular appetizer, served with sour cream and raw onion, as is the potato pancake with fried kielbasa or pierogi. Word to the wise: don't fill up on these initial offerings; there's lots more to come with the main dishes.

First-timers may wish to try the Polish Platter to get a sense of the quality and variety of Staropolska's home cooking. The platter features a little bit of everything—stuffed cabbage, mashed potatoes, kielbasa, hunter's stew, pierogis, and a potato pancake. Polish kielbasa is another good entrée choice. The sausages are served fried or boiled

Top left: Staropolska is the premier Polish restaurant in New Britain's Little Poland enclave.

Above left: A plate of pierogis—with cheese, meat, fruit, potato, or mushroom/sauerkraut filling—is an essential part of the Staropolska experience.

Top right: Start your meal with some fresh-baked bread and a cup of pickle soup.

Above right: Staropolska's Polish Platter provides a little bit of everything.

and come with a side of sauerkraut. And every night, a rotating roster of excellent specialties, mostly beef and pork dishes, are offered up from the kitchen.

There's a nice little patio alongside the restaurant with umbrellaed tables and Italian lights that's a great place to dine seasonally. Let Staropolska be your restaurant of choice whenever you seek fine Polish fare in Connecticut.

252 Broad St., New Britain; 860-612-1711
staropolska.net

"Tu Jadamy Jak U Mamy" is the restaurant's motto, which translates as "The way your mother used to do it."

Wining, dining, and boat-watching on New England's largest river

The lower Connecticut River valley is one of the most scenic parts of the state. A great place to enjoy its verdant beauty is at the funky, fun Blue Oar restaurant on the banks of the Connecticut River in Haddam.

In 1997, Jim and Jody Reilly first laid eyes on the somewhat dilapidated riverside building tucked into the woods. It was a faded gray structure on stilts next to a marina. They somehow saw a restaurant in its bones, and a month later they were serving up food in their spruced up eatery.

The Blue Oar is not an easy place to find. There's a hand-painted sandwich board sign at a bend along Connecticut Route 154 that reads, "Blue Oar: Eat by the River," and points down a bumpy road to a boatyard on the western bank of the river. After you cross the Essex Steam Train tracks and pass by the boatyard, you'll find yourself at the threshold of the restaurant, partially camouflaged by overhanging trees.

The restaurant's grounds are populated with colorfully painted picnic and café tables and chairs, adding a wonderful splash of color to the scene. Virtually all the seating is outdoors, with the exception of several stools along a counter rail on the restaurant's balcony.

The menu is displayed on blackboards tacked to the front of the yellow-hued cook shack. After you've made your selections, proceed up the outdoor stairs to the cook shack's wraparound deck and head inside to place your order.

The menu is eclectic. Burgers are very popular and come in several varieties, including bleu and Cajun cheeseburgers. Various chicken sandwiches and wraps, as well as a very nice grilled portabella sandwich with roasted red pepper aioli, provide options for non-beef

Left: Picnic tables scattered around the grounds can each accommodate several people.

Top middle: The Blue Oar, tucked into its verdant spot on the Connecticut River.

Above middle: The Blue Oar's signature Mandarin Salad.

Top right: A Blue Oar cheeseburger with all the trimmings.

Above right: One of the Blue Oar's colorful decks, overlooking the dock and the river.

and vegetarian diners. The Blue Oar does a nice, hot lobster roll that pairs well with a cup of creamy clam chowder. And perhaps the best item on the menu is the mandarin salad—chilled field greens with mandarin orange slices, raisins, walnuts, crumbled bleu cheese, and a tangy, homemade balsamic vinaigrette.

A local bakery trucks in all sorts of wonderful desserts daily, such as Key lime mousse, strawberry-rhubarb crumb tart, cookies, brownies, and pies. Reggae and other laid-back tunes are piped in, adding to the overall, relaxing atmosphere. But the best part is just sitting along the river, especially on a breezy summer evening, and watching the boat traffic and wildlife.

16 Snyder Rd., Haddam; 860-345-2994
blueoarct.wixsite.com/ctrestaurants

This little hideaway is a favorite of locals, who bring coolers of beer and wine (it's BYO). Boaters on the river tie up to the Blue Oar's dock and stop in for a meal or to grab carryout.

TANGIERS INTERNATIONAL

A culinary crossroads in Hartford's West End

"Specialty Foods for All People" is the owners' mantra at this popular international market and cafe located on Farmington Avenue in Hartford's West End. There's no place quite like it anywhere else in the state, and Tangiers customers come from near and far to shop and dine at this food emporium.

Founded in 1995 by a husband-and-wife team, Tangiers has been run by 4 of the couple's 11 children for the past decade. The Latif brothers share equally in the work and the rewards of their highly successful establishment. They also engineered Tangiers's 2014 move from its original location in West Hartford to its current location several blocks to the east across the Hartford city line.

When you enter Tangiers International, you're confronted with a sea of freestanding, brightly lit chrome shelves packed with foodstuffs from around the globe, particularly those from the Middle East and the Mediterranean. The "specialty foods for all people" come from such disparate lands as Lebanon, Israel, Greece, Italy, Jordan, Turkey, Armenia, Persia, India, Macedonia, Bulgaria, and Egypt. Though many of these countries may from time to time be at swords' points back home, their foodstuffs sit comfortably side-by-side in this warm, friendly marketplace.

Wander through the shelves and behold the amazing variety of products offered. There are several different types of tahini, olives, dates, dried fruits, rice of every kind, pasta, beans, grains, honeys, jams, and much more. There are also fresh produce and dairy sections and several cases of frozen foods from all over the world.

There's one other mantra at Tangiers that's been practiced since day one: "We bring peace through peoples' stomachs."

Top left: The gorgeous layout of the Tangiers shopping floor is irresistible to lovers of Middle Eastern and Mediterranean foods.

Above left: There's no end to the canned, jarred, fresh, and frozen foods to be found at Tangiers.

Middle: The chicken curry with chickpeas is served over rice pilaf and makes for a hearty, satisfying meal.

Top right: Tangiers is renowned for its delectable, eye-catching falafel sandwich.

Above right: The somewhat understated storefront gives little hint of the delights to be found inside Tangiers.

In a back corner of the market, there's a small lunch-counter café that serves a limited but flavor-packed menu of Middle Eastern dishes and snacks for dining in or for carryout. The counter is usually manned by one or two of the Latif brothers, who love interacting with their customers.

The most popular dish is the falafel: fried chick peas slathered with tahini and rolled with fresh vegetables in chewy, flavorful pita bread. Gyros, chicken kebab, and *kefta* kebab are other sandwich offerings. Meals served over rice pilaf include chicken curry with chickpeas, a lima bean stew with lamb, and baked stuffed eggplant. Small plates of hummus, tabouli salad, and baba ghanoush, all served with pita, make for great snacks.

550 Farmington Ave., Hartford; 860-233-8168
tangiersmarket.com

SUPER DUPER WEENIE

Silly name, superb hot dogs and fries

From humble beginnings as a food truck, Super Duper Weenie has grown into a hot dog powerhouse in Fairfield County. Some hot-dog aficionados consider Super Duper's weenies the best in the land. Roadfood's Michael Stern has always been a big fan, and Super Duper Weenie is also a favorite of Guy Fieri from *Diners, Drive-Ins and Dives*.

Owner Gary Zemola hunted down the truck, which he had frequented during his days in Norwalk in the 1980s, purchasing and refurbishing it in 1992. With a background in culinary arts, Zemola began developing recipes for various types of hot dog creations based on his interpretations of different types of weenies from all over the country. He also concocted his own relishes, sauces, and other condiments, and he decided that splitting and grilling the franks would be the Super Duper way. Fresh-cut-daily French fries also became a menu staple for the truck, and the formula for success was in place.

Zemola also took on a couple of partners from his neighborhood, John and Lorin Pellegrino. The resurrected food truck took to the streets, and the response from everyone was unconditional love. The decision was made in 2000 to create a "world headquarters" for the operation in the form of a brick-and-mortar stand on Black Rock Turnpike in Fairfield. Zemola attempted to retire the truck but met with much resistance from customers, so both operations continue to this day.

The menu at Super Duper is deep, varied, and fun. Start with the best-selling hot dog: the New Englander. This split-and-grilled wiener is dressed with sauerkraut, bacon, spicy mustard, sweet relish, and raw chopped onion. Then there's the New Yorker, which comes with sauerkraut, homemade onion sauce, mustard, and hot relish.

You may tour the nation's hot dog landscape with the Chicagoan (lettuce, tomato, mustard, celery salt, hot relish, and a pickle slice); the Californian (homemade meat chili, chopped raw onion, American cheese,

Top left: Super Duper Weenie started as a food truck in 1971, and a storefront restaurant opened on Black Rock Turnpike in 2000.

Above left: The famed New Englander dog, with sauerkraut, bacon, mustard, relish, and chopped onion.

Top middle: The massive griddle and deep fryers behind the order counter are a beehive of activity throughout the busy day.

Above middle: Super Duper's "world headquarters" consists of a bright, red order counter and an adjacent dining room.

Right: The Dixie Dog, which features meaty homemade chili and coleslaw.

and hot relish); the Dixie (meat chili and coleslaw); the Georgia Red Hot (a spicy Southern sausage covered in sauerkraut, mustard, and sweet relish); and the Cincinnatian (Cincinnati-style chili, cheddar cheese, and chopped onions). All hot dogs are served on soft, lightly grilled buns custom-baked just for Super Duper.

The burgers here are equally enthralling, as are the seasonal homemade soups. All these goodies are available from the truck or at world headquarters. What are you waiting for?

306 Black Rock Tpke., Fairfield; 203-334-3647
superduperweenie.com

Super Duper dispatches a truck to western Massachusetts every couple of months to procure the special potatoes used in their super-duper fries.

No advertising? No problem. Those in the know go to Clamp's.

Way up in the northern reaches of New Milford sits Clamp's Hamburger Stand, open every spring and summer since 1939. There's no phone, no website, and no big sign on Route 202 indicating it's there. Clamp's has existed, thrived acually, on word of mouth and a fiercely loyal customer base.

The roadside stand was founded by Edwin and Sylvia Clamp in front of their home. It didn't take long for curious locals to start patronizing the place, and locals have been the core of Clamp's business ever since.

The little white shed with its weathered blue awning is flanked on both sides by shaded picnic areas with tables, benches, and room to lay out a blanket to sit on. There's no indoor seating, so it's best to visit when the weather is fair.

Clamp's menu offers standard roadside grub, such as grilled hot dogs, a fish sandwich, grilled cheese, clam strips, fries, and chicken tenders. But the burgers are what Clamp's is all about. Made with freshly ground beef from a local butcher shop, the burgers ooze delightful trickles of juice onto the buns, adding to the honest flavor of these delectable patties.

The Clamp's business card reads: "NO SIGN, NO ADDRESS, NO PHONE, JUST GOOD FOOD." There used to be a sign, but it blew down decades ago and was never replaced.

Top left: Clamp's diminutive shack with its distinctive blue awning.

Above left: There are lots of lovely places to sit and enjoy your meal at Clamp's.

Right: Clamp's famous burger with all the trimmings.

A couple of things to know in advance: Clamp's is cash-only, and its hours of operation are a bit unorthodox (11 a.m. to 2 p.m. and 5 p.m. to 8 p.m. daily), presumably to give the owners and workers some siesta time in the middle of their busy days.

518 Litchfield Rd., New Milford

Lobster rolls, mulch, and so much more

There aren't many places where you can pick up ornamental trees and shrubs for the yard, a hanging plant for the porch or patio, and a lobster roll, hot dogs, smoothies, and ice cream for you and the kids. Jessica's Garden delivers all this and more and is well worth a visit for your gardening and gustatory needs.

Owner and founder Jessica Carroll is a highly credentialed landscape designer who has won awards for her work at the famed TPC River Highlands golf course in Cromwell. Jessica's Garden, located behind a modest pink house on Route 66 in Marlborough, reflects the landscape designer's love of nature and her desire to create a space where homeowners can pick up some garden goods and families can gather for an outdoor meal or snack.

Picture a backyard playground populated with pink-hued sheds, a disused greenhouse labeled county jail, numerous mismatched picnic tables and Adirondack chairs, a rope swing, and kitschy yard sculptures, all scattered around a small scenic pond. There's also a short path into the woods that leads to a "fairy garden." Kids love roaming around the grounds, and, for adults, there's a garage full of hanging plants, indoor and outdoor planters, and other gardening supplies.

One of the pink sheds serves as Jessica's snack shack and has a menu board tacked to the front next to the order window. Hot buttered lobster rolls are the main draw here, served in a grilled, buttered, top-split New England–style bun. Choose between a bag of chips or fresh cucumber slices for a side dish. (Cold, "Massachusetts-style" lobster rolls are also available.) You may fancy up your lobster by getting it on a grilled, buttered croissant for a couple of dollars more.

Top left: Whimsical artwork on the side of the food shack.

Above left: Chilled lobster salad with lettuce on a buttery croissant roll.

Top middle: Jessica's backyard is a playground for children and adults alike.

Above middle: Jessica's Garden has a little bit of something for everyone.

Right: Grilled, spicy *chouriço* sausage on a toasted bun.

Gourmet grilled cheese sandwiches are also popular. Try the chicken pesto, the chicken sundried tomato, the buffalo chicken bacon, the Green Garden Girl (spinach, sundried tomato, onion, and pesto mayo), or the Pig Pile (pulled pork, bacon, onion, and barbecue sauce).

Split hot dogs are grilled and served on toasted, buttered buns with the usual choice of toppings (get the hot pepper relish); and there's a 2 Dog Special that comes with chips and soda for less than 10 bucks. The lobster bisque and clam chowder are both excellent, and there are several different types of smoothies for the health-conscious.

Good news: Jessica's serves Gifford's Ice Cream from Maine, an increasingly popular treat in Connecticut.

198 E. Hampton Rd., Marlborough; 860-295-1685
jessicasgarden.net

There are four different types of smoothies to choose from and five "smoothie enhancers"–hemp protein, chia seeds, fresh ginger, flax seeds, and local honey–to mix in for optimum healthy goodness.

The corned beef hash and hash brown potatoes are to die for.

A long a busy stretch of Southbury's Main Street South, there's a nondescript, whitewashed, one-story building that houses one of the best diners in the state. The Laurel Diner has been wowing locals and diner aficionados for years with their world-famous corned beef hash and hash brown potatoes, and the rest of the menu is full of more surprises.

There has been a diner on this spot since the late 1940s under a succession of owners, each going for 15 years or so before selling and moving on. The Homicks, who bought the Laurel in 1997, are currently in their third decade of ownership with no signs of slowing down. It's a happy partnership between owners and townies that makes the Laurel a cherished community gathering place.

The focal point of the diner is the griddle, manned by Peter Homick, just across the counter and in full view of nearly everyone in the establishment. Homick deftly flips pancakes and burgers, puts crispy edges on corned beef hash and hash browns, fries eggs, folds omelets, and performs numerous other culinary tasks that produce consistently outstanding diner fare.

Take the hash as an example. Peter started with canned corned beef hash when he first purchased the Laurel, and over time he developed his own custom version. Once or twice a week, he cooks his own 30-pound brisket, along with carefully selected potatoes and chopped onions. The rest of the ingredients are a well-kept secret.

Laurel Diner owner Peter Homick and his wife, Stephanie, deserve the credit for making this eatery one of the best places to have breakfast in Connecticut.

Top left: The modest, whitewashed diner belies the amazing grilled treats to be found within.

Above left: The diner's famed corned beef hash, equally great as a side dish or a meal unto itself.

Top right: A typical breakfast plate with an order of hash browns on the side.

Above right: Peter Homick, owner and master of the griddle at the Laurel.

Once mixed, the hash blend is crisped up on the griddle and served as a side dish or on its own.

The Laurel Omelet is another menu highlight. Made with locally grown vegetables, many of which come from the Homicks' home garden, this treat features fresh spinach and mushrooms, roasted red bell peppers, and crumbled feta cheese. It pairs very nicely with crispy home fries hot off the griddle.

Grilled cinnamon rolls and cinnamon raisin French toast are other popular breakfast treats, especially with kids. On the lunch side, the BBQ, bacon, and onion-ring burger is tops, along with grilled, footlong Hummel hot dogs and a killer Reuben sandwich. Daily specials are written on the whiteboard walls, along with other dishes. Diner fare doesn't get much better than this.

544 Main St. South, Southbury; 203-264-8218
thelaureldiner.com

CAPTAIN SCOTT'S LOBSTER DOCK

A solid seafood shack amid boats and trains

Wedged onto a spit of land between the Amtrak train tracks and a commercial boat marina near downtown New London, Captain Scott's Lobster Dock is a highly likable seafood shack in an unlikely spot.

The seafaring Captain Scott of yore is best known for an act of bravery in 1870, in which he used his body to plug a hole in a sinking ferry boat docked in New York's North River, saving the lives of dozens of passengers. His heroism landed him in Ripley's Believe It or Not, where he was given the nickname "The Human Cork."

The layout of Captain Scott's Lobster Dock is linear, in keeping with the long, narrow shape of the property. First, there's the cedar-shingle shack, with its order and pick-up windows facing downtown New London. In front of that are a dozen or so open-air picnic tables, followed by a shingled, open-air pavilion with another 18 picnic tables, followed by an additional 10 alfresco tables and a bandstand on the other side of the pavilion—all lined up in shotgun fashion.

Lobster leads the list of goodies here, with dinners that feature a steamed lobster (choose your size), accompanied by corn on the cob, red potatoes or French fries, and coleslaw. Steamer clams are also available if you want to make it a true New England "shore" dinner. There's also a tasty lobster bisque, with big chunks of lobster meat in a creamy, sherry-infused broth.

Captain Scott's famous lobster rolls come in both hot and cold styles and in two sizes. The hot version, which is the most popular, features fresh chunks of warm lobster meat bathed in melted butter and served on a toasted bun. The cold roll features chilled lobster

Top left: You can reserve one of Captain Scott's food trucks to cater your special event.

Above left: Hot (*left*) and cold (*right*) lobster rolls, side-by-side. You can get both kinds at Captain Scott's.

Top middle: Captain Scott's light, flaky fish-and-chips.

Above middle: There's all sorts of great seafood to be had at Captain Scott's, including whole lobster dinners.

Right: Captain Scott's is one of the premier seafood shacks on the Connecticut Shore.

meat tossed in mayonnaise, a small amount of finely diced celery, and a dash of pepper. It's also served on a toasted bun that's lined with a crispy piece of lettuce. The large roll (hot and cold) has four ounces of meat in a footlong bun, and the smaller version has about an ounce less of meat and comes on a standard hot dog roll.

Co-owner Sue Tierney says the fish-and-chips dinner is one of the most popular items from the deep fryers. All the deep-fried seafood dinners, which come with red potatoes or fries and coleslaw, are more than reasonably priced, which makes this place popular with seafood-hungry families. BTW, Captain Scott's is BYO.

80 Hamilton St., New London; 860-439-1741
captscottsnl.com

Be sure to check out the small ice cream stand next to the food windows. It serves Gifford's ice cream, a real treat from central Maine. It's a great way to cap off a wonderful seafood experience.

With roots dating back to the American Revolution

Touting itself as one of the country's oldest continuously operating country inns, the "Gris," as it's affectionately known to locals, has all the trappings of a classic colonial restaurant and taproom. With its wall-to-wall hangings of nautical paintings, its wood-burning fireplaces, and its maritime decor, this place is as much a feast for the eyes as it is for the palate.

Getting its start in 1776, the Gris initially housed and fed shipbuilders who flocked to Essex at the beginning of the American Revolution. During the War of 1812, the British sailed up the Connecticut River and burned the American ships and ship works in Essex, but the Gris kept its doors open. The steamboat era of the 1800s brought new prosperity to the town and the inn, and today the Gris is wildly popular with people from all over the Northeast.

When you step into the dimly lit main dining room, you're immersed in a glorious time gone by. The wooden tables and hand-crafted wing chairs set the stage for a variety of historic meals at different times of the year. The 1776 Sausage Sampler—three different types of sausage served with Dijon mustard—is a great way to start your repast. Baked cod, pan-seared scallops, butternut squash ravioli, and roasted prime rib of beef with horseradish lead the offerings for entrées. Panko-encrusted fish-and-chips is a good choice for lunch. Be sure to wash it down with one of the many craft beers on draught.

The Sunday Hunt Breakfast is a year-round bacchanalia of a buffet that changes seasonally yet regularly features such delicacies as freshly baked corn bread and scones, omelet and waffle stations,

Top left: Potato cakes with apple sauce and sour cream are a great opener.

Above left: The Griswold Inn at the base of Main Street in Essex.

Middle: There are always plenty of interesting brews on tap at the Gris.

Top right: The main dining room is awash in nautical-themed artwork.

Above right: Faroe Island salmon with herbed basmati and soy-glazed Brussels sprouts.

pecan and caramel French toast souffle, herb-roasted chicken, and chocolate brownie pudding.

Christmas is a special time at the Gris when seasonal game such as goose, boar, quail, and venison appear on the menu, and costumed carolers stroll the dining rooms, taking requests from patrons. And it's "Sea Chantey Night" Monday evenings year-round in the uber-charming taproom, where The Jovial Crew performs seafaring ballads to enthusiastic crowds. Be sure to get there early, as the intimate room fills quickly prior to the 8 p.m. start time.

A stroll up and down Essex's Main Street is a perfect adjunct to a visit to the Gris. It's every bit as charming as the inn itself.

36 Main St., Essex; 860-767-1776
griswoldinn.com

In recent years, the Gris opened a lovely wine bar in an adjacent historic building where they offer a tapas-style menu along with their fine wines.

QUAKER DINER

A classic diner in upscale West Hartford

West Hartford is well known for its many hip restaurants, bars, and specialty food shops. The Quaker Diner is definitely a throwback to a different time, yet it offers a nice counterpoint to the town's trendier offerings.

Housed in a one-story, barrel-roofed brick building, the Quaker came into being in 1931. Unlike many diners of the time, the Quaker wasn't factory-built and shipped to the site. It was designed by a Hartford architect and built by a local construction company. The diner underwent extensive renovations in 1987 but still looks much the way it did when it first opened.

Breakfast is the big meal here, and it's served all day until the diner closes in the early afternoon. Though the dishes are quite basic, they're all well prepared, many of them on the griddle in full view of stool jockeys. The French toasts are noteworthy, as are the omelets, particularly the smoked turkey and the feta, spinach, and tomato versions.

Lunch features burgers, tuna and patty melts, and a very nice grilled ham and cheese sandwich. Specials are posted above the grill, handwritten on pieces of paper. Be sure to check out all the memorabilia on the walls while you're there. The place has quite a history.

319 Park Rd., West Hartford; 860-232-5523

The Quaker Diner originally had a glass-topped counter. The space beneath the countertop was refrigerated for cold food and beverage storage.

Top left: The brick, barrel-roofed Quaker Diner on Park Road in West Hartford.

Center left: The Quaker's famous French toast, swimming in a sea of syrup streaked with butter.

Above left: The diner's interior, with many of its original design elements.

Top right: The Quaker Diner's menu with a photo of founder Aristides "Harry" Bassilakis.

Above right: The diner's backsplash with locally made Avery's Soda on display.

A great place for a cone, a sundae, or a dairy barn tour

Thank goodness this place is open to the public because the ice creams churned out by the University of Connecticut School of Agriculture are perhaps the best frozen treats in the entire state. Ask any UCONN student or recent grad about this campus oasis, and chances are eyes will glaze over and go into a dreamlike state—such is the power of the confections that come from this year-round frozen-treat paradise.

The Dairy Bar opened in 1953 as an offshoot of the UConn Creamery, part of the school's department of animal science. The Creamery has been producing milk from the school's herds since the early 1900s, and a portion of the milky harvest was put into producing top-quality ice cream. You can see ice cream being made at the Dairy Bar through plate glass windows that overlook the production area. It's quite an education, and the payoff comes when visitors order up and slurp down the ice cream of their choosing.

There are 24 standard flavors and a number of seasonal flavors that rotate throughout the year. Peach ice cream is a summer special; followed by cinnamon caramel swirl, pumpkin, and maple walnut in the fall; and then peppermint stick in wintertime. By far, the favorite year-round flavor is Husky Tracks, a blend of vanilla ice cream, large chunks of Reese's Peanut Butter Cups, and swirls of fudge.

The Dairy Bar itself is brightly colored, with an L-shaped order and service counter, numerous tables, flat-screen TVs, and whimsical art on the walls. The space gets lots of natural light from floor-to-ceiling glass along a couple of the walls.

In addition to sugar, safety (flat-bottomed kind), and waffle cones, there are one- , two- , and three-scoop sundaes of the ice creams of

Left: The UConn Dairy Bar's sunny facade beckons students and others to come in and enjoy some of the best ice cream in the state.

Middle: A typical small sundae topped with homemade whipped cream.

Top right: There is a revolving menu of ice cream flavors that should satisfy even the most persnickety customers.

Above right: Hard ice cream is hand-scooped out of chilled barrels the old-fashioned way, with lots of skill and a strong wrist. Students hold most of the counter service jobs.

your choosing. All the toppings, including whipped cream, jimmies, gummy bears, and crushed candy bars are available for slight upcharges. All the ice cream treats here are very affordable, making this ice cream mecca all the more appealing.

Nearby barns and on-campus pastures welcome visitors in-season to observe dairy cows grazing and being milked. There's also a Dairy Bar ice cream truck that makes the rounds on campus and is available for appearances at special events.

There's no need to wait for summer. Head on over to the Dairy Bar year-round to enjoy the best this fine dairy outlet has to offer.

17 Manter Rd., Storrs; 860-486-1021
dining.uconn.edu/uconn-dairy-bar/

LIUZZI GOURMET FOOD MARKET

If it's Italian, Liuzzi's has it.

Italian Americans and many others from all over the state flock to this one-of-a-kind food market in North Haven that offers the most authentic, most imported, most truly Italian foodstuffs to be found in Connecticut.

Brothers Pasquale and Nicola Liuzzi initially opened the store in 1981 and started selling their homemade cheeses, which Pasquale had learned to make while managing C&F Cheese in East Haven. Liuzzi's homemade mozzarella and ricotta cheeses started winning awards, and the brothers haven't looked back. Many family members have joined the business, along with Liuzzi's professionally trained staff.

The market has an L-shaped floor plan that's easy to follow. Don't be surprised if you leave with far more purchases than you intended to make. Everywhere you turn, there are delectables calling your name from shelves and glass-fronted cases.

Walk through the front door, and you're face-to-face with the deli section, offering hanging Parma hams, salamis, smoked sausages, and meats galore sliced to order behind the counter. Liuzzi's imports traditional dried and cured meats from all over Italy, and they also offer a vast array of Boar's Head cold cuts. Additionally, there are olives, roasted red peppers, marinated eggplant, stuffed peppers and anchovies, and other antipasto dishes.

Cheeses are next. Liuzzi's offers more than 200 different types from all over the world, with an emphasis on Italian cheeses. In addition to the award-winning mozzarella and ricotta, you'll find wheels of Parmigiano and other Italian specialties such as Burrata, Caciocavallo, and Scamorza. Spanish and French cheeses are also stocked in abundance, as are many goat's milk cheeses of varying provenance.

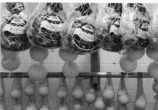

Top left: Liuzzi's store shelves are packed with all sorts of tempting imported goodies from Italy and elsewhere.

Above left: Liuzzi's storefront on State Street in North Haven.

Middle: Wheels of Reggiano Parmigiano cheese are an ever-present sight in the cheese section.

Top right: Home-baked mac and cheese can be found in the prepared foods section.

Above right: Parma hams and balls of cheese hang from the wall in the deli section.

There's a full-service butcher's department with all cuts of beef, veal, chicken, and pork, custom-cut to your particular needs. Liuzzi's beef carries the "Certified Black Angus" label, one of the few places in the state with such a quality designation.

Next is the sandwich stand, where you can grab a premade sandwich or custom order one to your liking. There are hot and cold varieties with, of course, an emphasis on Italian favorites such as capicola, *soppressata* (a dry italian salami), meatball, provolone, and eggplant parmesan.

Then there are the groceries—cans and jars and packages of tomatoes, pastas, olive oils, cookies, balsamic glazes, and more—beckoning from wire shelves scattered throughout the market. With all this, you'll think you've died and gone to Italian heaven.

322 State St., North Haven; 203-248-4356
www.liuzzimarket.com

Shoppers get misty-eyed when they come here, thankful for the bounty of Italian gourmet treats to be found within Liuzzi's four walls.

East meets West in this marriage of cultures and cuisines.

This Szechuan/Chengdu Chinese restaurant was born out of love and longing. In 1995, Chinese national Hu Ping traveled to Singapore to learn English. Her teacher was Jonathan Dolph of Madison, Connecticut. The two married a year after meeting and immigrated to the United States in 2000. Frustrated that she couldn't find any authentic Chinese food on the Connecticut Shore, Hu convinced Jonathan to quit his job, and they bought Taste of China on Post Road in Clinton, where Hu proceeded to transform the menu into what many consider to be the best Chinese cuisine in the state.

Taste of China is a truly remarkable and unique place, with its elegant dining rooms, its expansive menu, its cozy bar, and its broad selection of Belgian beers, a favorite libation of Jonathan's. The dining rooms have been refurbished recently and look even more inviting than ever, with round, dark wood tables centered by lazy susans for convivial family and large-group dining. Several booths and plenty of glass-topped tables are also at the ready for smaller parties.

The printed menu at Taste is a sight unto itself. More than a dozen pages long and filled with color photos of many of the dishes, it's equally informative and tempting. Take your time while perusing, and don't hesitate to ask the restaurant's knowledgeable staff for explanations and recommendations.

The appetizers menu features several nontraditional standouts, such as ginger-flavored string beans, served perfectly cooked and then chilled in a light ginger sauce; and the sliced beef with Sichuan

Eight different types of Belgian beers are served at Taste of China.

Top left: Taste of China's recently refurbished main dining room is warm and inviting.

Above left: Bento boxes are a great choice for lunchtime.

Top right: Sizzling Shrimp and Scallops comes with loads of snow peas, mushrooms, bamboo shoots, and onion on a sizzling platter.

Above right: One of the top appetizers is the sliced beef with Sichuan pepper and chili.

pepper and chili, a slightly hot dish with thin-sliced beef sauteed with onions, bell peppers, carrots, and chili peppers in a tangy brown sauce. The hot and sour soup is also an excellent starter.

Entrée choices number more than 30, with many interesting dishes you won't find many other places. For instance, try the whole sea bass braised in a spicy red soybean sauce; the "Ants Crawling on Trees" (mung bean noodles with ground pork and spices); the Tangerine Beef, breaded and deep-fried, then bathed in a tangy orange sauce; and Ma La Duck, smoked duck mixed with peanuts and peppers. Sauteed string beans (again, served chilled) is a standout vegetable entrée.

This is a great place to come with a group and experience the breadth and depth of Szechuan and Chengdu cuisine while quaffing a Belgian ale in a warm and inviting atmosphere.

233 E. Main St., Clinton; 860-664-4454
tasteofchinaus.com

Burgers done in a truly unique fashion

This is the place where they say the hamburger was invented. A ground beef patty served between two pieces of toasted white bread is founder Louis Lassen's original sandwich, and it's still served the same way to this day. Whether or not it's the first, it's truly an original, and it's a fascinating window into the culinary past, both in Louis's presentation and method of cooking.

The story goes that Lassen owned a food cart on the streets of New Haven in the late 1800s. He began adding lunch items to his standard stock of dairy products. In 1900, a hungry customer implored Lassen to throw together something tasty and quick that the customer could take with him, and the first Louis' Lunch hamburger sandwich was the result.

Today, Louis' Lunch is housed in a quaint, cramped brick building with Tudor-style windows on Crown Street. It can hold only slightly more than a dozen or so customers at a time in its dimly lit interior. Walk through the front door and behold the order counter with four stools on one side and wisecracking owner Jeff Lassen and an assistant on the other.

Besides the counter stools, there are several wooden, alcove-like seats that look a lot like monks' stalls in a medieval cathedral. There are a couple of other tables, one large, one small, and that's about it. "Cozy" doesn't begin to describe the feeling one gets when dining here.

Ordering is fairly simple: step up to the counter and let Jeff and his staff know how many burgers you want. Choices are limited. Burgers are served on toasted white bread with onion, sliced tomato, cheese spread, and that's it. No ketchup, no mustard, relish, or other condiments. All burgers are made from five types of beef ground fresh daily and are only cooked medium rare. As for sides, you may

Left: Burger sandwich assembly occurs behind the counter, right before customers' hungry eyes.

Middle: The Louis' Lunch Hamburger sandwich, in all its simple, tasty glory.

Top right: Lucky customers can grab a stool at the order counter and watch the show in the cramped kitchen area.

Above right: Louis' Lunch's distinctive exterior has a certain Tudor feel to it and brightens up its stretch of Crown Street in New Haven.

choose between a cup of homemade potato salad, potato chips, and homemade pie. Signs above the counter help guide you through the ordering process.

With regard to cooking, the burgers are inserted into a vertical gas broiler that harkens back to the early 1900s and that looks like something from your grandparents' (or great-grandparents') kitchen. The slices of bread are toasted in a 1929 radiant gas toaster, and the hamburgers are quickly assembled next to these relics. Foxon Park soda (several flavors) is the beverage of choice.

261 Crown St., New Haven; 203-562-5507
louislunch.com

No ketchup served here. Don't even ask.

BLACK EYED SALLY'S

Fine southern barbecue and live blues at this downtown Hartford mainstay

Long before the current barbecue craze swept the state, Black-Eyed Sally's opened its doors (and its barbecue pits) in 1995, a welcome beacon of Southern cooking in Connecticut's capital city. Founder James Farano took a research trip to Memphis in the mid-1990s and returned to Hartford with a head full of ideas and a notebook full of recipes.

Housed in a 100-year-old brick building on downtown's Asylum Street, Farano has expanded Black-Eyed Sally's over the years. It currently holds a dining room, a music room, and upstairs and downstairs bars. Each of the rooms is filled with colorful artwork depicting blues and jazz musicians and ephemera redolent of life in the South. Live music is featured six nights a week, making Sally's a must-stop for blues musicians and fans from around the country.

The barbecue at Sally's is substantial, high quality, and reasonably priced. In addition, there are numerous other examples of southern cuisine, such as jambalaya, gumbo, and red beans and rice from New Orleans; blackened catfish from Cajun country; and numerous great side dishes such as molasses-infused collard greens, melt-in-your-mouth corn bread, and house-made barbecue potato chips.

Sundays are a great time to visit for Sally's Southern Brunch, often accompanied with gospel performances to lift the spirit while satisfying your culinary cravings.

350 Asylum St., Hartford; 860-278-7427
blackeyedsallys.com

Left: Folk art and portraits of blues and jazz musicians liven the walls throughout Sally's.

Top right: A plate of Sally's barbecued chicken, ribs, homemade coleslaw, and red beans and rice.

Above right: Black-Eyed Sally's smoky exterior beckons to all those craving tasty barbecue and great live music.

From the get-go, Sally's has played host to some of the best blues musicians in the world, who consider it a must-stop when performing in the Northeast.

High-end, innovative cuisine in a beautifully restored mill

When Millwright's burst upon the Connecticut restaurant scene in 2012, it was an immediate sensation and has been drawing raves from diners and critics ever since. Housed in a beautifully restored 1600s mill building with a waterfall on Hop Brook in Simsbury, the restaurant's setting is almost as inspiring as the food that comes from talented chef/owner Tyler Anderson.

There's a lot going on at Millwright's, starting with the mesmerizing pond and waterfall around which the mill is built. Sitting next to the waterfall is the main dining room, with floor-to-ceiling glass to gaze upon the watery scene. There's another view from a narrow bridge that passes over the stream below the falls and that has several private dining alcoves with bird's-eye views of the falls. Back in the main building, one floor below the main dining room, there's the 1630 Tavern, a less-formal eatery that also has windows onto the rushing waters. And there are tables outside across the bridge for seasonal dining and great views of the red-hued mill building.

On to the food: The menu is an ever-changing carousel of innovative offerings, many based on inventive riffs on traditional New England foods. For instance, a recent second-course offering was tapioca, the pudding infused with all the flavors one associates with thick, creamy clam chowder. Then there's chicken and dumplings, featuring dumplings in the form of ricotta gnocchi and enhanced with root vegetables and smoked chicken. (Smoked meats make all sorts of splendid appearances on the menu at any given time. There's a large smoker on one side of the building next to the front door and parking lot.)

Left: The colorful pedestrian bridge also houses several tables.

Top middle: Millwright's main dining room.

Above middle: Grilled mahi mahi with coconut curry on a bed of jasmine rice, pecans, and golden raisins.

Top right: Tuna tostada.

Above right: The 1680 Tavern, one level below the main restaurant.

Patrons in the dining room typically have a choice between a four-course dinner (two courses of small plates, an entrée, and dessert) or a seven-course chef's tasting menu that changes constantly and may be accompanied by beverage pairings with each course. The menu in the tavern is a la carte and features many of the small and large plates available in the dining room plus a couple of different burgers, a chicken sandwich, chicken wings with a dipping sauce, and oysters by the half-dozen.

Should you choose to dine outdoors in season, there are yet more different menu offerings—things such as alpine cheese fondue with apples, croutons, pearl onions, and smoked pork belly; and gourmet s'mores for dessert. (Once again, it's a four-course meal).

This is a really fun, scenic, and vibrant place to enjoy a truly unique cuisine, where every visit will bring new surprises to even the most jaded diners.

77 West St., Simsbury; 860-651-5500
millwrightsrestaurant.com

Two stories of lobster fun on the East Haven waterfront

This magnet for hot buttered lobster rolls recently moved from its charming red trailer in a Branford marina to a newly refurbished building next to the waterfront in neighboring East Haven. Owners Arlene and Nick Crismale miss their old home in Branford, where they built a large following of loyal locals, but they're doing great in their new spot, which has both indoor and outdoor seating on two levels. Theirs is a story of love and loss and love resurrected, seafood shack style.

Nick Crismale was a lobsterman and commercial clammer for many years on Long Island Sound. He always wanted an informal seafood shack on land, but his wife was doubtful. Long story short: Nick went ahead and bought a used trailer in the early 2000s and then outfitted it to serve a limited menu of seafood and wieners. Arlene was tasked with running it, and an unlikely love affair between shack and owner blossomed. The Crismale's had to make the hard decision to move to a new location a couple of years ago when they couldn't come to a lease renewal agreement with their Branford landlord, landing on their feet in neighboring East Haven.

The new shack is situated on a beach road between Long Island Sound and some wetlands, with a tidal creek running between the two on one side of the lobster-red, two-story building. Enter through the front door and behold the clever chalkboard menu wrapping its way around the kitchen order window.

Lobster rolls are the main draw, and they come in two sizes: regular (approximately four ounces of lobster) and "The Whaler" (half a pound). The lobster is warm and buttered with a spritz of lemon and is served on toasted sub rolls. There are two other lobster

Left: Locally made Foxon Park soda is served in a variety of flavors.

Top middle: Two warm, buttered lobster rolls.

Above middle: The recently relocated Lobster Shack in its new East Haven home.

Right: A split and grilled wiener and an Italian sausage with onions and peppers.

sandwiches to consider: the Lobster Toasted Cheese (lobster meat with Havarti cheese on buttered sourdough bread) and the Lobster 'n Land (a grilled hamburger on a brioche bun with Havarti cheese and fresh lobster), a unique twist on surf and turf.

There are three types of chowders: creamy New England, clear-broth Rhode Island, and creamy shrimp and corn. Locally made Foxon Park soda is the beverage of choice. There are several types to choose from. The shack is BYO for alcohol.

Not to be overlooked are the sausage, peppers, and onions on a toasted sub roll and the split and grilled Hummel hot dogs, hailing from nearby New Haven. French fries and onion rings are ideal sides with any sandwich or roll.

Grab a seat indoors or out, on the deck or alongside the parking lot, and enjoy the sea breezes that waft in from the Sound on sunny summer days.

3 Cosey Beach Ave., East Haven; 203-483-8414
lobstershackct.com

TED'S STEAMED CHEESEBURGERS

The nexus of the steamed cheeseburger universe

Central Connecticut is ground zero for steamed cheeseburgers. In fact, it's just about the only place in the world where you can get them. Meriden is the unofficial capital of this culinary phenomenon, and Ted's is probably the best place to go for a true steamed cheeseburger experience.

First, a bit about the origins and nature of the steamed cheeseburger. It's believed that the first steamed cheeseburgers were made at a Middletown lunch spot called Jack's. Proprietor Jack Fitzgerald rigged up a steam box to cook the beef and melt the cheese for his burgers. Each burger patty and chunk of cheese has its own separate compartment in the steam box, the belief being that the steam draws out the fat and retains the juiciness of the burgers. This same basic cooking method is used by steamed-burger vendors throughout the region.

Ted's opened its doors in 1959 and is in its third generation of family ownership. It's housed in a tiny, house-type building on Meriden's Broad Street just north of downtown. The interior consists of three booths and a counter with about 10 stools. On the other side of the counter are a few stainless-steel steam boxes, a small deep fryer, an even smaller griddle, a soda dispensing machine, a cash register, and a small bench for sandwich prep. Every square inch of the space is used in the cooking process.

The beef used in the burgers is ground fresh daily and packed into small, rectangular steaming pans that each hold one burger. The same goes for the cheese, a special type of cheddar that remains a secret

Left: The sign over Ted's is easy to spot when driving on Broad Street.

Top middle: Ted's tiny interior is cramped and convivial.

Above middle: Ted's famous steamed cheeseburger, topped with veggies and oozing melted cheese beneath.

Right: One of Ted's seasoned cooks, flying the company colors.

held by Bill and his family. The rectangular pans slide into racks inside the steaming box, which is fired by gas burners over large pans of water. Grease from the burgers drips down and is drained away, and the cheese melts into a mouthwatering blob of gooey flavor.

When burgers and cheese come out of the steamers, they're paired with soft-roll buns and toppings that include lettuce, tomato, raw or grilled onion, bacon strips, and more. The preferred side dish is Ted's home fries—thick-cut potatoes deep fried and crisped up on the griddle.

There's more on the menu, but the steamed cheeseburger is what this place is all about. Give it a try, and you'll dream for days afterward about the beefy, gooey-cheesy bliss of Ted's famed steamed cheeseburger.

1046 Broad St., Meriden; 203-237-6660
tedsrestaurant.com

MODERN APIZZA

This famed New Haven pizzeria is modern in name only.

Located on State Street just a few blocks away from the Wooster Street neighborhood, Modern Apizza carved out its identity and took the name "Modern" in the 1940s. Initially owned by a string of neighborhood locals, Modern was eventually purchased in 1988 by Billy Pustari. Along with his wife, he built Modern into the pizza juggernaut it is today.

Modern is a double storefront. One side contains the fabled gas-fired oven and booths for diners, while the other side has seating up front and a very busy carryout area in the back.

Modern's signature dish is a true "apizza" (pronounced (a-BEETS)—a thin, light pizza with a slightly burnt crust around the edges. The basic pie is tomato sauce atop crispy crust with a dusting of parmesan cheese and a sprinkling of olive oil. From this base, Modern's pizzas blossom into a multitude of variations.

Pies come in small (12-inch), medium (16-inch), and large (18-inch) sizes, the latter big enough to feed four hungry people, especially if preceded by Modern's hefty Caesar salad, also appropriate for sharing. Garlic bread with mozzarella slathered on top is another popular appetizer, as is bruschetta, a seasonal treat.

The massive oven is a sight to behold, so be sure to check it out sometime during your visit. Pies are inserted and maneuvered around with long-handled wooden paddles deftly operated by Modern's staff.

This is the only one of New Haven's "big three" pizzerias that's not on famed Wooster Street, but that in no way diminishes its standing in the world of New Haven–style pizza.

Left: Modern's massive gas-fired oven produces dozens of pizzas every day.

Top middle: Modern Apizza's sign and awning on New Haven's State Street is a welcome site for pizza lovers.

Above middle: A sausage and mushroom pie.

Top right: The Caesar salad is a great opener and more than enough for two.

Above right: Locally made Foxon Park soda is the beverage of choice at Modern.

Pizza toppings include your choice of all the popular types (sausage, pepperoni, onion, mushroom, red bell peppers, anchovies, and more) as well as more exotic ones such as anchovies and hot cherry peppers.

Specialty pies are the best way to go. The clam pizza, made with fresh-shucked littleneck clams, is world-famous, as is the clams casino version, which includes bacon and roasted peppers. The eggplant pizza is delightful, especially if you get it with bacon sprinkled over the top. The Italian Bomb (bacon, sausage, pepperoni, mushroom, onion, peppers, and garlic) and the Veggie Bomb (spinach, broccoli, olives, mushrooms, onions, peppers, and garlic) are for those who want it all.

The waitstaff is friendly and efficient and will attend to your every need. Modern certainly has earned its crown as one of the top three pizzerias in the Elm City.

874 State St., New Haven; 203-776-5306
modernapizza.com

A beautifully maintained 1950s diner in Connecticut's Quiet Corner

Just a stone's throw from I-395 in northeast Connecticut, Zip's Diner is a glorious step back in time to when highways were lined with stainless-steel, factory-built diners serving piping-hot comfort food to weary travelers.

Zip's in its current location dates back to 1954, when the Jerry O'Mahony diner was shipped to Dayville and plopped down at the intersection of routes 12 and 101 (I-395 didn't yet exist). At that time, route 101 was a major connector between Hartford and Providence, Rhode Island.

The diner is named after retired Connecticut state trooper Henry "Zip" Zerher, who originally owned the diner when it was in nearby Danielson several miles to the south of Dayville. Conrad and Olive Jodoin purchased the Dayville diner from Zerher in 1960, launching a family dynasty of Jodoin ownership that is currently in its third generation.

Perhaps the most famous and iconic thing about the diner is the monolithic neon EAT sign that towers some 15 feet above the roofline. It has been the subject of admiration among diner aficionados and makes occasional appearances in Bill Griffith's "Zippy the Pinhead" comic strip. The diner's interior is lovingly maintained in its pristine original condition.

Many famous people have stopped at Zip's over the years, including ballplayers Ted Williams, Joe DeMaggio, and Carl Yastrzemski, and entertainers Liberace and, more recently, Renée Zellweger.

Left: Many of the fixtures on the interior of Zip's are originals, or, like the counter stools, lovingly remade versions of the originals.

Top right: Zip's meals are served on charming China plates and bowls, adding to the nostalgic feel of the place.

Above right: Zip's is a shining example of a beautifully maintained O'Mahony diner from the 1950s.

With regard to food, it's pretty much standard diner fare—bacon, eggs, sausage, corned beef hash, omelets, pancakes, burgers, sandwiches, meatloaf, and more. If you want to go full-on New England, try the Yankee Pot Roast at dinnertime.

Other good choices include the turkey, roast beef, and meat loaf platters, diner classics that include two slices of open-face bread, gravy, mashed potatoes, and vegetables.

725 Hartford Pike, Dayville; 860-774-6335
zipsdiner.com

An ice cream stand and so much more

This legendary clam shack sits on the floodtide of the Mystic River along Route 1 as the road winds eastward to nearby Stonington. The fried clams here pull in locals as well as hordes of tourists motoring north on nearby I-95. It's well worth the detour off the interstate to enjoy some of Connecticut's finest deep-fried seafood.

The Sea Swirl was once a Carvel Ice Cream stand, and it shows in the architecture—the sloped roof and the three glass sides—not to mention the soft-serve ice cream machines just behind the order counter. Ice cream (soft-serve and hand-scooped) still plays a major role here, but the Swirl's reputation these days is mostly due to the deep fryers.

Dave and Kathleen Blaney bought the ice cream stand in 1984 and transformed it into a clam shack with ice cream on the side. They developed their own recipes, breading certain seafood in flour or cornmeal and dipping other types in the wet batter. This gave their seafood offerings amazing variety.

The Blaneys sold Sea Swirl to longtime customer Mark Adams, who has been running it with his family for the past 10 years. The formula remains basically the same. The whole-belly clams are dredged in flour, the clam strips and scallops in cornmeal, and the cod in wet batter. The oil in the fryers is changed frequently, guaranteeing fresh flavor.

Start your meal with an order of six clam fritters—fried balls of dough flecked with minced clam. They're great for dipping into a cup or bowl of creamy or clear-broth clam chowder. The whole-belly clams and clam strips are popular main dishes, as are the fish-and-chips and the sea scallops, both bought locally from the fishing fleets out of nearby Stonington harbor. Clam rolls and the cod fish sandwich are faves with many regular customers.

Left: Sea Swirl stands out on Route 1 in its converted Carvel ice cream building.

Top right: Step right up and order any or all of these tempting treats at this dine-in-the-rough diamond in the rough.

Above right: The fish-and-chips at Sea Swirl are renowned for their crunchy crust and their sweet cod from nearby Stonington.

For those not inclined toward seafood, there are some great ⅓-pound hamburgers and cheeseburgers, split and grilled hot dogs, and chicken tenders. Chili is the topping of choice on the hot dogs, and grilled onions, peppers, or mushrooms dress up the burgers very nicely.

The ice cream offerings are seemingly endless, with soft-serve or hard-packed cups and cones, sundaes, flurries, shakes, and ice cream sodas.

Whether your tastes run to food or to ice cream (or both), there are plenty of picnic tables scattered around the grounds to enjoy your feast in the sunny oasis of this wonderful roadside eatery.

30 Williams Ave., Mystic; 860-536-3452
seaswirlofmystic.com

For many years, Sea Swirl opened on the first day of the Boston Red Sox season and closed after the Sox season ended.

VINNY'S ROAST BEEF AND DELI

This sandwich shop is the beating heart and soul of Wallingford.

If you're cruising down Central Street in Wallingford, it's impossible to miss Vinny's Roast Beef and Deli with its roast beef sandwich sculpture over the front door. There's also a life-sized fiberglass likeness of Elvis hanging from the side of the building. Pull into the narrow side parking lot, and you'll discover that the guitar-strumming King statue is augmented by outdoor speakers blaring Elvis hits throughout the day. Someone here loves the Big Guy, and the smart money is on the deli's high-octane owner, Vinny Iannuzzi.

Iannuzzi opened his namesake roast beef stand in 1982. The focus of Vinny's menu is its award-winning array of roast beef sandwiches. Iannuzzi seasons, tenderizes, and then slow-cooks each of his roasts overnight. The cooked roasts are brought into the deli, sliced paper-thin behind the counter glass, and then loaded onto bread or a roll.

The sandwiches come in an array of types and sizes, many with clever names, such as the All Nighter (hot roast beef, homemade horseradish, and au jus on a kummelweck or grinder roll), the Serenity (hot beef, bacon, and horseradish), the Rancher (roast beef, Monterey Jack cheese, barbecue sauce, and coleslaw), or the Sinus Relief (roast beef, swiss cheese, horseradish, and jalapeno peppers). You may, of course, get a straight-up roast beef on rye with lettuce and tomato, as well as just about any custom roast beef sandwich you can come up with.

Other sandwiches of note outside the realm of roast beef include the Mario Lanza (meatballs, pepperoni, and ricotta and mozzarella cheeses), the Gino (chicken breast, prosciutto, and spinach with

Left: The walls at Vinny's are plastered with all sorts of sports memorabilia and photos of local public and private school youth sports teams.

Top middle: Vinny's always has a $9.99 hot buttered lobster roll, available year-round.

Above middle: One of the deli's many facades from days gone by. (Courtesy of Vinny's.)

Top right: Vinny's signature sandwich, which may be had in more than a dozen different variations.

Above right: Elvis holds sway over the side parking lot with his guitar, sideburns, and speakers blaring Elvis hits on a continuous loop.

Caesar dressing), the Sophia Loren (roasted turkey with thinly sliced prosciutto, lettuce, tomato, and mayo), and the Sylvester Stalami (salami, ham, provolone, sliced hot peppers, and marinated eggplant). All come in either kummelweck or grinder rolls and are, of course, made to order.

Vinny is a huge supporter of the local community through youth team sponsorships, food donations to first responders, and so much more. He's also a big "Made in the USA" booster, purchasing all his foodstuffs and other products within the nation's borders. He's built a huge local following, and there's always room for more.

567 Center St., Wallingford; 203-265-7288
vinnysdeli.com

Vinny's has seasonal wild game offerings in its sandwiches and stews, such as wild boar, venison, and Cajun alligator (pieces of tail meat breaded, fried, and served in a sandwich).

A hip spot for lovingly made northern Indian food

This bohemian-style Indian eatery combines great food with an intimate, relaxed atmosphere in a quiet, small-town shoreline location. Himalaya opened with a quiet splash in late 2017, and it became an almost instant sensation with fans of great Indian food and curious locals in search of a new dining experience.

Himalaya is well thought out in both its decor and its menu. It occupies a small space in a nondescript building that backs up to a motel on Route 1 in Old Saybrook. The interior is playfully decorated with rough-hewn wooden tables and furniture along with lots of embroidered throw pillows, a comfy couch, and twisty decorative wooden poles fastened to the walls. There's an L-shaped bar with half a dozen stools that overlook Himalaya's small open kitchen. Bollywood films are often projected on one of the restaurant's blank white walls. The overall atmosphere is cheery and intimate.

The menu at Himalaya is traditional and experimental at the same time, and it changes frequently, with certain dishes coming and going and coming back again. Start your meal with a basket of crispy *papadum*, made from black graham flour and cumin, perfect for dipping into one of several chutneys offered on the menu. Himalaya's flavorful mulligatawny soup makes regular appearances, as does the intoxicatingly fragrant appetizer Patra—Colocasia leaves rolled with chickpea flour, herbs, and spices, steamed and cut into bite-size portions.

Main dishes alternate between the traditional and the exotic. For instance, Himalaya's chicken tikka masala features large chunks of chicken breast immersed in a smooth sauce of tomatoes, warm herbs and spices, and cream. It rivals the tikka masala in any highly regarded city restaurant.

Left: Chicken Biryani served over fragrant basmati rice.

Top middle: Himalaya Café's inviting storefront on Post Road in Old Saybrook.

Above middle: A basket of papadum, made from black graham flour and cumin, gets things started.

Top right: Himalaya's funky, fun dining room makes customers of all stripes feel at home.

Above right: Himalaya's Nine Jewels Korma is a vegetarian's delight.

There are various dishes bathed in korma, an aromatic, cashew-based sauce with a touch of cream and golden raisins blended in. Of particular note is the Nine Jewels Korma, a vegetarian delight chock-full of fresh organic produce and chickpeas.

Salmon—not often found on many Indian menus—is a mainstay here. There's Salmon Korma, Salmon Tikka Masala, Salmon Vindaloo, and more. And from the tandoori oven come Himalaya's famous Tandoori Chicken, two types of naan, and a vegan roti.

Be forewarned that most dishes here are quite spicy, so ask for low-to-no spice if you're so inclined. (You'll still feel some heat with their most modest seasonings.) Himalaya is a real shoreline gem, so pay them a visit if you're looking for some excellent, home-cooked Indian food.

1456 Boston Post Rd., Old Saybrook; 860-577-5300
himalayacafeoldsaybrook.business.site/

TAINO SMOKEHOUSE

A standout on the Connecticut barbecue scene

Barbecue is a relative newcomer to the New England dining scene, and perhaps the best place for it in the Nutmeg State is Taino Smokehouse of Middletown. Housed at one end of an Ace Hardware building about a mile outside downtown, Taino is a diamond in the New England barbecue rough.

The restaurant's founder, Chris Szewczyk, quit his office job a little over 10 years ago and took several road trips through various barbecue hot spots (Texas, Kansas City, and Alabama among them); then, he developed his unique mix of barbecue styles using his Ole Hickory Pits smoker. He and his wife, Jenny, opened Taino in 2012 to great acclaim and the delight of many in the Middletown and Wesleyan communities.

The name "Taino" is that of an indigenous tribe in the Caribbean. The Taino practiced "barabicu," the method of cooking meats in a fire pit; the term seemingly found its way into the Spanish language as "barbacoa," and then into English as "barbecue." The restaurant pays homage to this ancient tribe through its name and its cooking methods.

Taino's indoor space is dark and comfy, with only half a dozen tables and an order counter that handles lots of take-out business. When things warm up outdoors, Taino opens its expansive outdoor flagstone patio on the side of the building, with its numerous picnic tables and its wood-stoked outdoor grill and smokers.

Taino recently opened a second location, Taino Prime, in Meriden, where the specialties are dry aged steaks and grilled salmon in addition to barbecue.

Top left: Platters of barbecue and sides: pulled chicken and pork, brisket, coleslaw, creamed spinach, and fresh-baked corn bread.

Above left: Beef brisket, pulled pork, and pulled chicken sandwiches are served on brioche buns.

Top right: Taino's distinctive logo is painted on the side of the restaurant.

Above right: A hefty platter of St. Louis pork ribs; marinated, smoked, deep-fried chicken wings; and sides of mac and cheese and coleslaw.

Perhaps the best way to experience Taino's range of barbecue styles and flavors is to go big and order one of the platters, which feature a choice of two or three meats, two to four sides, and two to four slabs of homemade corn bread. This is plenty of food for a few people.

From the smokers, choose between prime Texas-style brisket, barbecue chicken, pulled pork or chicken, and St. Louis spare ribs. The pulled chicken is a particular delight, moist and flavorful; the brisket tender; and the ribs rich and smokey. Sides include mac and cheese, coleslaw, collard greens, three types of French fries, and coleslaw.

Other menu highlights include marinated, smoked, deep-fried chicken wings for openers; burgers and sandwiches served on brioche buns and with homemade potato chips; and Taino's signature BBQ Egg Roll—a crispy tube stuffed with smoked chicken, red peppers, mashed potatoes, and mac and cheese.

Enjoy this cornucopia with five different types of homemade barbecue sauces, and you'll scratch your barbecue itch happily at Taino's.

482 S. Main St., Middletown; 860-358-9828
tainosmokehouse.com

WESTFAIR FISH & CHIPS

A local favorite of deep-fried-seafood lovers

Located in a tiny strip mall behind some stores fronting Post Road in Westport, Westfair Fish & Chips has been serving up deep-fried goodness for more than 35 years, a testament to the quality of their simple yet highly desired fare in this upscale community.

Westfair occupies two small storefronts in the strip mall. One of them is the kitchen, and the other is a small dining room with an order window. When it's your turn to order, be sure to check out the bins of flour for breading that sit in front of the deep fryers. Everything is made to order, which takes some time but is well worth the wait. The menu is posted on the wall. Carryout is a big part of Westfair's business, but it's a fun place to sit and dine for a quick meal indoors or outside at the adjacent picnic tables.

The main show is, of course, the namesake fish-and-chips. Served piping hot from the kitchen's deep fryers and hand-breaded per order, the fish's crispy, crunchy exterior is perfectly paired with the sweet, tender cod within. Flounder is also available for an upcharge. Other deep-fried fare includes whole-belly clams, clam strips, sea or bay scallops, shrimp, oysters, and sole.

Three types of clam chowder are offered as well as a hot buttered lobster roll, but deep-fried seafood is what this place is about, and the fish-and-chips are tops in the region.

1781 Post Rd. East, Westport; 203-255-3184
westfairfishandchip.com

Top left: A basket of Westfair's signature fish-and-chips, made from fresh cod, breaded and fried to order.

Above left: The wall-mounted menu gives any seafood lover plenty to ponder.

Right: Westfair's modest storefront operation belies the great fried seafood within.

Westfair has a lobster tank brimming with red guys that are cooked to order, along with steamers, chowder, and other delicious side dishes.

GUILFORD LOBSTER POUND

Lobster rolls from a bona fide lobster fisherman

When you want to get a hot buttered lobster roll in Connecticut, it's best to head to the shore along Long Island Sound and seek out a special spot such as the Guilford Lobster Pound. Owned by lobsterman Bart Mansi, this little shack and deck on the water is a great place to enjoy a roll, some chowder, stuffed clams, a bag of chips, and any sort of beer or wine you want to bring to the party.

Mansi has been lobstering on Long Island Sound since the mid-1970s, and he purchased the Pound in 1991. He uses the dock and shack as his base of operations, including his cold-water tanks for lobster storage. Most days, he leaves the dock at 4 a.m. to check on his traps in the sound, returning home in the afternoon to offload his catch.

In 2008, Bart rebuilt the dock, added a bunch of umbrellaed picnic tables, and opened his lobster roll stand with lots of help from his wife, Janice, and their daughter. Open from mid-May to mid-October, the Guilford Lobster Pound has gained a reputation as one of the best places in the state to get a lobster roll.

A metal pushcart anchors the food service area at the base of the dock. Janice and her servers assemble the lobster rolls, wrap them in foil, and whisk them to eagerly waiting customers. Each roll contains a quarter pound of fresh-picked lobster meat that's been bathed in butter and tucked into a toasted, buttered, split-top bun. A bag of chips and a soda round out the standard meal, but there's more to enjoy if you're interested.

First, consider the clear-broth clam chowder, made fresh in the shingled shack daily. Each serving is chock-full of fresh clams, tender potatoes, and Italian seasonings. It's a great complement to the lobster rolls, especially if there's a cooling breeze coming in off the water.

Top left: A lovely hot buttered lobster roll ready to go.

Above left: Many of the picnic tables offer a great view of the adjacent salt marsh, a popular spot for bird-watching.

Top right: The lobster pound's deck has plenty of open-air picnic tables for dining by the water.

Above right: The clear-broth clam chowder is chock-full of clams, potatoes, and lots of seasonings.

In recent years, a friend of Bart's has been supplying the Pound with stuffed clams, which are typically served as appetizers. These "stuffies," as they're referred to in Rhode Island, consist of minced clams, bread stuffing, and spicy sausage blended together and baked in a large, quahog clam shell. It's a great way to start or supplement a lunch or dinner on the dock and a real taste of southern New England shore life.

505A Whitfield St., Guilford; 203-453-6122
guilfordlobsterpound.com

Bart Mansi owns a 42-foot-long lobster boat, the *Erica Page* (named after his daughter), which he keeps moored to the Guilford Lobster Pound dock.

Innovative dining in a historic home

Metro Bis chef/owner Chris Prosperi is legendary in the Connecticut restaurant scene, universally liked and respected and with good reason. As reporter Joseph Montebello of *The Litchfield County Times* pointed out in a column last year, "The first time you meet Chris Prosperi, it's like running into an old friend."

Schooled in engineering at UConn, Chris gravitated to cooking when he took a job as sous-chef at West Street Grill in Litchfield in 1991. He and his wife bought Metro Bis (which translates to "Metro Encore,"—the restaurant was an extension of Metro Kitchen, a restaurant in Granby) in 1998. The Prosperis moved Metro Bis to an 1820s house in Simsbury in 2013, then moved once again to its current location in the historic Joseph Ensign House in 2018. The brownstone mansion was built in 1906 by Ensign, who owned the adjacent munitions factory.

The setting is nothing short of gorgeous, with an expansive dining room and banquet facility on the first floor and a lovely deck overlooking the spacious lawn surrounding the building. Prosperi's cookery these days may best be described as New American, yet there are still French inflections in much of the cooking. Prosperi presides over the kitchen, which may be partially viewed from the lovely dining room.

The menu at dinner these days is a four-course, prix-fixe celebration of all that Prosperi has learned through his years of cooking and culinary arts teaching, much of it done on radio and television. The first course features a choice of such regular items as crispy cauliflower and pan-seared crab cake along with seasonal specials such as acorn squash with honey, sage, and pumpkin seeds. Next up are the soups and salads, with a fine arugula salad, a beet

Left: Warm lighting and rich color tones dominate Metro Bis's dining room.

Top center: Chocolate rhubarb sundae, with shaved chocolate and whipped cream.

Above center: The alluring service bar beckons from the back of the dining room.

Right: Braised chicken with polenta, roasted broccoli, and a smoked jalapeno demi-glaze.

salad with smoked tomato and goat cheese, and, once again, seasonal specials such as chilled asparagus with a creamy herb vinaigrette and a butternut squash bisque.

Fish and fowl dominate the third (main) course with such seasonal offerings as braised chicken, eggplant and zucchini, pan-seared striped bass, and spaghetti squash with brussels sprouts.. The dessert course is an ever-changing selection of sundaes, tarts, and fresh sorbets.

Simsbury is very lucky to have Chris and his talents in their midst, and they reward him with a full house nearly every night. (There is a similar three-course meal offered at lunchtime.)

690 Hopmeadow St., Simsbury; 860-651-1908
metrobis.com

For many years, Chris was the weekly senior contributor on the highly popular "Faith Middleton's Food Schmooze" radio program on WNPR.

GLENWOOD DRIVE IN

A time-tested fast-food stand that delivers on flavor and festivities

Serving up top-notch hot dogs, hamburgers, and other quick foods to the denizens of Hamden for more than 60 years, the Glenwood Drive-In is synonymous with good, old-time food and fun that hearken back to simpler times.

Owned by Rocky Stone and his progeny since 1955, Glenwood has deep roots in the community. The roadside stand has changed its exterior look several times over the decades, but everyone in town knows where it is and what it stands for: great fast food, helpful service, and a focal point for the town's families and local workers.

The Glenwood experience starts with gazing at the colorful, wall-mounted menu advertising all that the drive-in has to offer. First, there are Glenwood's famed char-grilled hot dogs, which hang off both ends of their top-split bun. They come in several varieties enhanced with cheese, chili, bacon, grilled onions, and more. The Glenwood also has its own proprietary spiced relish, a favorite that locals load up on.

The burgers are hefty and made with fresh-ground Angus beef that's char-grilled to your liking. Deep-fried seafood is also popular, with whole-belly clams, clam strips, scallops, shrimp, and soft-shell crab (in season) offered, as well as a generously portioned hot lobster roll. (All seafood orders may be supersized to platter status for a nominal upcharge.)

Stop by Wednesday evenings April through October for the Glenwood's popular cruise nights. Locals bring in their jalopies, pop their hoods, and show off their rides in the parking lot.

Top left: The Glenwood's luminous order menu entices in many different ways.

Above left: Footlong wieners are char-grilled throughout the day.

Middle: A black cherry fudge ice cream cone from Kelly's Cone Connection.

Top right: A couple of footlongs dressed with mustard and the Glenwood's own spicy relish.

Above right: The Glenwood Drive-In has been a mainstay on Hamden's Whitney Avenue for more than 60 years.

    With regard to sides, go with the onion rings, which are hand-cut and lovingly breaded throughout the day. They're crispy, crunchy, and full of fresh fried onion flavor. A solid second choice is the sweet potato fries.

    Be ready to order quickly when you're here. Next to the wall-mounted menu stands an employee with a computer monitor to record your order and tally up your bill. After your order is in the system, move down the line to the food pickup area, which stands next to the grill, deep fryers, and cash register. You'll be asked what you ordered, so do your best to remember. It's a bit confusing but part of the Glenwood's charm.

    After you've got your food on a plastic tray, stop by the condiments stand for the hot relish, ketchup, mustard, and raw onions. Grab a table back in the dining room or sit at one of the numerous stools lining the front windows overlooking the street. Be sure to save room for ice cream at the companion Kelly's Cone Connection adjacent to the dining room.

2538 Whitney Ave., Hamden; 203-281-0604
glenwooddrivein.com

A mom-and-pop eatery befitting of its Washington Depot surroundings

This little café in the charming village of Washington Depot is situated in a small shopping center in the central business district. It's the preferred gathering place for residents and tourists seeking lovingly made meals and baked goods or just a cup of coffee or a glass of wine and some local camaraderie.

Established in 1977 by Michael and Nancy Ackerman, this quaint eatery and gourmet foods shop changes its menu almost daily with a rotating lineup of soups, quiches, salads, sandwiches, and cheese boards that pair very nicely with a glass of wine at lunchtime. The Pantry's interior is a mix of tables for dining and chrome shelving filled with gourmet foods (many from Italy) and housewares of all sorts.

Baking has been an important part of the business from the beginning, and there's a tempting display case of cookies, cakes, breads, and rolls separating the kitchen from the dining area.

Menu highlights include carrot ginger soup, finback cheese from Mystic, spinach and cheddar quiche, and various ham and turkey sandwiches served on homemade bread or a spinach wrap. Save room for one of the home-baked desserts such as flourless chocolate torte, carrot cake, or caramel pecan brownies.

If you happen to live not too far away, consider having The Pantry cater any event you may have in mind. They're known for

The Pantry regularly offers Mediterranean goodies such as hummus, baba ghanoush, Moroccan eggplant, and yogurt dip from the famed restaurant Oliva on Main in nearby Bethlehem.

Top left: The Pantry mixes dining and shopping in a fun and festive atmosphere.

Above left: Ginger carrot soup and some bread and cheese make for a delightful lunch.

Top right: The bakery case is a cornucopia of sweet and savory baked treats.

Above right: A watercolor rendition of The Pantry's quaint exterior. (Courtesy of The Pantry.)

their inventive menus and timely delivery and service. From 2 to 20 persons and more, The Pantry can help wow your guests with inventive and healthy appetizers, meals, and desserts.

5 Titus Rd., Washington Depot; 860-868-0258
thepantryct.com

A 90-year-old diner that wears its age and its history very well

This shoebox-size Tierney diner is wedged at an angle between two larger buildings on Winsted's main drag, and it's been there since 1931. The Winsted has a long and storied history, which owner Asa Flint is more than happy to share with patrons. This place is so small (just a dozen or so stools) that it's virtually impossible to have a private conversation, but the community chatter is part of the fun.

The barrel-roofed diner was shipped from the O'Mahony factory in New Rochelle, New York, in 1931 and placed on the concrete foundation where it still sits today. The Winsted survived the big flood of 1955 and a fire in 2005. Many original features of the original diner remain intact. It has long been a focal point in Winsted's pretty downtown, and folks gather here for good conversation and good food.

The small diner griddle sits right across from the counter. Asa mans the griddle seven days a week, churning out breakfast and lunch and, occasionally in the summer, barbecue at his few outdoor tables on the covered side patio.

Flint prides himself on his hot dogs and bratwurst, best enjoyed with homemade chili, sauerkraut, and barbecued onions on top. Breakfast must-haves include the corned beef hash and cheese omelet and the unusual pancake sandwich—scrambled eggs, cheese, and a breakfast meat of your choosing encased between two fluffy flapjacks.

496 Main St., Winsted; 860-379-4429
winsteddiner.com

Left: The diner's tiny interior makes for cozy conviviality between owner and customers.

Top right: A typical Winsted Diner breakfast—plain, simple, and irresistibly good.

Above right: The tiny, weathered Winsted Diner stands proudly (if a bit askew) on Winsted's Main Street.

In 1973, Bob and Carol Radocchio purchased the Winsted Diner and operated it 24 hours a day, 7 days a week, for the next 32 years, with lots of help from their five children.

A time-honored way to enjoy the bounty of the Connecticut River Valley

For more than 60 years, the Rotary Club of Essex has been putting on a highly unusual and entertaining event. The Essex Shad Bake, held late spring in the charming Connecticut River town of Essex, celebrates the locally famous fish with a one-day festival filled with food, drink, live music, and educational presentations.

The Essex Rotary Club Shad Bake began in 1958, when scores of fishermen still went out on the river at night to lay drift nets for shad. The bake was just one of several similar events along the river to showcase country-style traditions to curious visitors to the Connecticut River Valley. The Rotary Club has remained a stalwart sponsor of the event since its inception.

For several weeks from late April to mid-June, the anadromous shad swim up the Connecticut River to spawn then return to the ocean. Though there aren't as many shad or fishermen as in years past, there's still plenty to keep the festivities going, and throngs of locals and tourists eagerly await the shad's springtime reappearance.

The shad bake typically occurs on the first Saturday in June, when shad are in the midst of migrating up from Long Island Sound and spawning in the Connecticut River. The one-day event is held on the grounds of the Connecticut River Museum, on the banks of the river at the foot of Essex's Main Street.

The fun begins when a large fire pit is set up next to the museum. A group of Rotary Club volunteers keeps the wood-burning fire going throughout the day, while other volunteers prepare the shad for baking. The fillets are individually nailed to oak planks, along with salt pork strips, which add flavor and lubrication to the cooking process. Olive oil is slathered on the fillets, followed by a dusting of bright-red paprika and other spices.

Left: Shad filets are nailed to wood planks and set out to cook by an open fire.

Right: Seasoned shad boards ready for placement next to the fire pit.

The planks are then positioned in a circular fashion around the scorching fire, and the fillets slowly bake for 15 to 20 minutes in the searing heat. When a batch of fillets is ready, a call of "Board!" goes up from one of the volunteer cooks. The shad planks are pulled away one by one from the fire and taken to a table where the nails are removed, and the fillets are whisked away to the dining tent.

While the shad are baking, there are lots of fun things to take in, such as a live demonstration on how to fillet shad. Each fish has hundreds of small bones, and it's an increasingly rare skill to be able to fillet shad quickly, efficiently, and properly before cooking.

All the Rotarians' hard work pays off when the shad is served up with a scoop of homemade potato salad, a generous helping of greens, a slice of pie, and a libation or two.

Connecticut River Museum, 67 Main St., Essex

rotaryclubofessex.com

The nearby town of Haddam has a Shad Museum that's open during shad fishing season and preserves the history of shad fishing in the Connecticut River Valley.

A longtime hangout for mariners in the Submarine Capital of the World

Sitting almost literally in the shadow of the massive Gold Star Bridge over the Thames River, Norm's Diner of Groton has borne witness to changes in community, clientele, and ownership over the past half century yet still stands, proudly shining on the road that leads to Groton's waterfront. This Silk City gem, manufactured in Paterson, New Jersey, in 1954, has been a longtime favorite of Groton's working class, especially laborers from nearby Electric Boat and swabbies from the submarine base just upriver near Gales Ferry.

Originally owned by Norm and Annie Brochu, the diner has had a few different owners over the past dozen years, but the menu has remained pretty much the same. The diner itself still has most of its original factory-made features, including the tile work, the stainless-steel cladding on the exterior, chrome backsplashes, colorful stools and counter, and the comfortable booths that are an important part of the diner experience.

Happily, Norm's still has its griddle just across the counter, where you may see your meal being prepared. There's also a kitchen in back for baking and roasting and doing the dishes, but having the griddle front and center is really a great throwback to what diners were all about.

Once a 24/7 operation, Norm's is now a breakfast and lunch spot only, with the exception of Saturday, when it stays open all night to accommodate the post-party crowd. Breakfast is served at all times, another diner hallmark.

The three-egg omelets come in a variety of combinations, freighted with such fillings as ham, cheese, sausage, bacon, mushrooms,

Top left: The diner's interior remains pretty much as it was when it was delivered nearly 70 years ago.

Above left: The griddle still sits just over the counter, where you can watch your meal being prepared.

Top middle: The ever-popular Norm's burger features Swiss cheese, bacon, grilled onions, and a pile of onion rings.

Above middle: Norm's Diner is a fine example of a Silk City diner car imported from the factory in Paterson, New Jersey.

Right: Norm's takes good care of its regular local customers and workers, the lifeblood of their business.

onions, bell peppers, and more. The Philly Cheese Steak omelet is particularly popular, as is the Mexican omelet, laden with salsa, cheese, chili, and jalapeño peppers.

Pancakes nearly hang off the edges of the plate, so ordering two is usually more than enough for a meal. If you really want to go to town, try the Pancake Sandwich, a belt-busting combination of two flapjacks with an egg in the middle and two strips of bacon on top. Breakfast sandwiches featuring an egg with ham, bacon, or sausage on a hard roll are also popular.

For lunch, try the Norm's Burger, a hefty beef patty adorned with Swiss cheese, bacon, and grilled onions with a hefty side of fried onion rings. The grilled sandwiches, like the patty melt, the Ruebens, and the grilled cheese, are other good options.

171 Bridge St., Groton; 860-405-8383

ZUPPARDI'S APIZZA

West Haven's contender for the crown of the state's greatest apizza

Though not in New Haven proper, Zuppardi's Apizza of West Haven serves up some excellent New Haven–style pizza and lots of other wonderful goodies. It's an excellent alternative to the crowds at the Elm City's big three pizzerias (Pepe's, Sally's, and Modern).

The establishment was founded as Salerno's Bakery on West Haven's Union Avenue in 1934, but Dominic Zuppardi eventually dropped the baked goods in favor of his increasingly popular thin-crust pizza and, in 1947, renamed it Zuppardi's Apizza. Currently, in its third and fourth generations of Zuppardi ownership and management, this is truly a family business success story.

Of the dozen or so specialty pizzas, there are three or four that really stand out. The Special, a red pizza with mozzarella, mushrooms, and Zuppardi's homemade fennel sausage, is perhaps the most popular. The Fresh Clam pizza features fresh-shucked littleneck clams on fresh dough with an intoxicating mixture of garlic and Italian spices. Then there's the Plain Pie, a classic "ah-beetz" with homemade tomato sauce, Pecorino Romano cheese, and fresh garlic if desired.

> One afternoon in mid-March 2021, two Secret Service agents showed up at Zuppardi's front door. They were there to pick up 10 pizzas for Vice President Kamala Harris and her entourage, who were in town to visit the West Haven Child Development Center. Co-owner sisters Lori and Cheryl Zuppardi were so thrilled they threw in an 11th pie for free.

Top: Zuppardi's colorful sign and awning herald the pizzeria's location in a residential, working-class neighborhood of West Haven.

Bottom: The Fresh Clam pie is the real deal, with generous amounts of fresh-shucked littleneck clams.

The best of the many good starters is the Antipasto Focaccia, Zuppardi's cold antipasto salad served atop warm garlic focaccia and covered with a generous sprinkling of shredded mozzarella.

179 Union Ave., West Haven; 203-934-1949
zuppardisapizza.com

RESTAURANTS A-Z

Abbott's Lobster in the Rough, 18
117 Pearl St., Noank

Antojos, 10
115 New Canaan Ave., Norwalk

Arethusa Farm Dairy, 14
822 Bantam Rd., Bantam

Atlantic Seafood Market, 42
1400 Boston Post Rd.,
Old Saybrook

B. F. Clyde's Cider Mill, 26
129 N. Stonington Rd., Old Mystic

Bill's Seafood, 46
548 Boston Post Rd., Westbrook

Bishop's Orchards, 50
1355 Boston Post Rd., Guilford

Black Duck Cafe, 62
605 Riverside Ave., Westport

Black-Eyed Sally's, 152
350 Asylum St., Hartford

Blackie's, 58
2200 Waterbury Rd., Cheshire

Bloodroot, 36
85 Ferris St., Bridgeport

Blue Oar, 126
16 Snyder Rd., Haddam

Bohemian Pizza and Tacos, 76
342 Bantam Rd., Litchfield

Bridgewater Chocolate, 70
559 Federal Rd., Brookfield
227 Federal Rd., Brookfield
12 LaSalle Rd., West Hartford

Bufalina, 104
1070 Boston Post Rd., Guilford

Captain Scott's Lobster Dock, 138
80 Hamilton St., New London

City Fish Market, 106
884 Silas Deane Hwy.,
Wethersfield

Clamp's 132
518 Litchfield Rd., New Milford

Corner Restaurant, 120
105 River St., Milford

Costello's, 74
145 Pearl St., Noank

Donahue's Clam Castle, 122
1324 Boston Post Rd., Madison

Doogie's, 118
2525 Berlin Turnpike, Newington

Dottie's Diner, 80
787 Main St. S., Woodbury

Essex Shad Bake, 184
Connecticut River Museum,
67 Main St., Essex

Flanders Fish Market, 78
22 Chesterfield Rd., East Lyme

Ford's Lobster, 110
15 Riverview Ave., Noank

Frank Pepe's Pizza Napoletana, 24
157 Wooster St., New Haven

Frog Rock Rest Stop, 30
212 Pomfret Rd., Eastford

Fromage, 102
873 Boston Post Rd.,
Old Saybrook

Glenwood Drive-In, 178
2538 Whitney Ave., Hamden

Goulash Place, 20
42 Highland Ave., Danbury

Grano Arso, 38
6 Main St., Chester

Griswold Inn, 140
36 Main St., Essex

Guilford Lobster Pound, 174
505A Whitfield St., Guilford

G-Zen, 68
2 E. Main St., Branford

Harry's Place, 52
104 Broadway St., Colchester

Heibeck's Stand, 44
951 Danbury Rd., Wilton

Himalaya Café, 168
1456 Boston Post Rd.,
Old Saybrook

Jessica's Garden, 134
198 E. Hampton Rd.,
Marlborough

Lakeside Diner, 48
1050 Long Ridge Rd., Stamford

Laurel Diner, 136
544 Main St. South, Southbury

Lilly's Soul Food, 66
305 Windsor Ave., Windsor

Liuzzi Gourmet Food
Market, 146
322 State St., North Haven

Liv's Shack, 114
26 Bridge St., Old Saybrook

Lobster Landing, 72
152 Commerce St., Clinton

Lobster Shack, 156
3 Cosey Beach Ave., East Haven

Log House Restaurant, 112
110 New Hartford Rd.,
Barkhamsted

Long Wharf Food Trucks, 82
351 Long Wharf Dr., New Haven

Louis' Lunch, 150
261 Crown St., New Haven

Makris Diner, 32
1797 Berlin Trpk., Wethersfield

Metro Bis, 176
690 Hopmeadow St., Simsbury

Mexicali Rose, 4
71 S Main St. #1, Newtown

Millwright's, 154
77 West St., Simsbury

Minas Carne, 34
36 Osborne St., Danbury

Modern Apizza, 160
874 State St., New Haven

Monkey Farm, 28
571 Boston Post Rd.,
Old Saybrook

Norm's Diner, 186
171 Bridge St., Groton

O'Rourke's Diner, 6
728 Main St., Middletown

Parkville Market, 8
1400 Park St., Hartford

Pho 501, 22
501 Main St. #5, East Hartford

Quaker Diner, 142
319 Park Rd., West Hartford

Rein's New York–Style Deli, 40
435 Hartford Trpk., Vernon

Roseland Apizza, 116
350 Hawthorne Ave., Derby

Sally's Apizza, 64
237 Wooster St., New Haven

Sea Swirl, 164
30 Williams Ave., Mystic

Shady Glen, 54
840 Middle Turnpike E.,
Manchester

Staropolska, 124
252 Broad St., New Britain

Sultan's Turkish Restaurant, 16
586 Plank Rd., Waterbury

Super Duper Weenie, 130
306 Black Rock Trpk., Fairfield

Sycamore Drive-In, 108
282 Greenwood Ave., Bethel

Taino Smokehouse, 170
482 S. Main St., Middletown

Tangiers International, 128
550 Farmington Ave., Hartford

Taste of China, 148
233 E. Main St., Clinton

Ted's Steamed
Cheeseburgers, 158
1046 Broad St., Meriden

The Pantry, 180
5 Titus Rd., Washington Depot

The Place, 2
901 Boston Post Rd., Guilford

Traveler Restaurant, 12
1257 Buckley Hwy., Union

UCONN Dairy Bar, 144
17 Manter Rd., Storrs

Union League Cafe, 56
1032 Chapel St., New Haven

Vinny's Roast Beef
and Deli, 166
567 Center St., Wallingford

Westfair Fish & Chips, 172
1781 Post Rd. East, Westport

Willimantic Brewing
Company, 60
967 Main St., Willimantic

Winsted Diner, 182
496 Main St., Winsted

Zip's Diner, 162
725 Hartford Pike, Dayville

Zuppardi's Apizza, 188
179 Union Ave., West Haven

APPENDIX

NEAR NEW YORK (FAIRFIELD COUNTY)

Antojos, 10

Black Duck Cafe, 62

Bloodroot, 36

Bridgewater Chocolate, 70

Goulash Place, 20

Heibeck's Stand, 44

Lakeside Diner, 48

Mexicali Rose, 4

Minas Carne, 34

Super Duper Weenie, 130

Sycamore Drive-In, 108

Westfair Fish & Chips, 172

THE LITCHFIELD HILLS (LITCHFIELD COUNTY)

Arethusa Farm Dairy, 14

Bohemian Pizza and Tacos, 76

Clamp's, 132

Dottie's Diner, 80

Log House Restaurant, 112

The Pantry, 180

Winsted Diner, 182

THE CAPITAL REGION (HARTFORD COUNTY)

Black-Eyed Sally's, 152

Blackie's, 58

Bridgewater Chocolates, 70

City Fish Market, 106

Doogie's, 118

Jessica's Garden, 134

Lilly's Soul Food, 66

Makris Diner, 32

Metro Bis, 176

Millwright's, 154

Parkville Market, 8

Pho 501, 22

Quaker Diner, 142

Shady Glen, 54

Staropolska, 124

Tangiers International, 128

YALE COUNTRY (NEW HAVEN COUNTY)

Bishop's Orchards, 50

Bufalina, 104

Corner Restaurant, 120

Donahue's Clam Castle, 122

Frank Pepe's Pizza Napoletana, 24

Glenwood Drive-In, 178

Guilford Lobster Pound, 174

G-Zen, 68

Laurel Diner, 136

Liuzzi Gourmet Food Market, 146

Lobster Shack, 156

Long Wharf Food Trucks, 82

Louis' Lunch, 150

Modern Apizza, 160

Roseland Apizza, 116

Sally's Apizza, 64

Sultan's Turkish Restaurant, 16
Ted's Steamed Cheeseburgers, 158
The Place, 2
Union League Cafe, 56
Vinny's Roast Beef and Deli, 166
Zuppardi's Apizza, 188

CONNECTICUT RIVER VALLEY (MIDDLESEX COUNTY)

Atlantic Seafood Market, 42
Bill's Seafood, 46
Blue Oar, 126
Essex Shad Bake, 184
Fromage, 102
Grano Arso, 38
Griswold Inn, 140
Himalaya Café, 168
Liv's Shack, 114
Lobster Landing, 72
Monkey Farm, 28
O'Rourke's Diner, 6
Taino Smokehouse, 170
Taste of China, 148

UCONN TERRITORY (TOLLAND COUNTY)

Rein's New York–Style Deli, 40
Traveler Restaurant, 12
UCONN Dairy Bar, 144

THE QUIET CORNER (WINDHAM COUNTY)

Frog Rock Rest Stop, 30
Willimantic Brewing Company, 60
Zip's Diner, 162

MYSTIC COUNTRY (NEW LONDON COUNTY)

Abbott's Lobster in the Rough, 18
B. F. Clyde's Cider Mill, 26
Captain Scott's Lobster Dock, 138
Costello's, 74
Flanders Fish Market, 78
Ford's Lobster, 110
Harry's Place, 52
Norm's Diner, 186
Sea Swirl, 164